W9-DBI-844

The Winter's Tale:
A Commentary on the Structure

The Winter's Tale:
A Commentary on the Structure

Fitzroy Pyle

NEW YORK
BARNES & NOBLE, INC.

First published by
Routledge & Kegan Paul Ltd., London, 1969

Published in the United States of America 1969
by Barnes & Noble, Inc., New York, N. Y.

© *Fitzroy Pyle* 1969

Printed in Great Britain

Contents

TO PECHA

Preface

This commentary has developed out of a paper read in 1940 on the unity of *The Winter's Tale*. That was a counterblast to Quiller-Couch's strictures on the play's 'faults and even absurdities of construction' (p. xx).[1] No such general defence is necessary today. Already in 1942 F. R. Leavis was saying that 'Properly taken, the play is not romantically licentious, or loose in organization'. Yet eight years later it was still possible for Clifford Leech to write of *The Winter's Tale*, along with *Pericles* and *Cymbeline*, as works of 'haphazard structure, exemplified notoriously in the convenient devouring of Antigonus, with the craftsmanship of individual scenes varying from the highest to almost the lowest' (*Shakespeare's Tragedies*, p. 135). However, when in 1958 Nevill Coghill remarked, 'It is a critical commonplace that *The Winter's Tale* is an ill-made play', it was only the more conveniently to devour the proposition; and since then John Lawlor (1962), J. H. P. Pafford (1963) and Ernest Schanzer (1964) have strongly defended the construction. Nevertheless, that the play is *well* made is by no means yet a critical commonplace. The full beauty of its plotting remains to be recognized.

A related 'platitude of criticism'—as D. G. James put it in 1937—'that the later plays are the writings of a man careless of what he is doing' (p. 207), has, I believe, been more tenacious of life. That Shakespeare in the Romances 'can even be careless' (J. F. Danby, p. 107)—that there are in *The Winter's Tale* loose

---

[1] E.g. the disparate nature of its two 'halves', hopelessly botched together, the huddled-up jealousy of Leontes, the scamping and complete mismanagement of the scene of recognition between himself and Perdita, the uneconomical final exit of Antigonus, the failure to make Autolycus 'a factor in the plot'. To this most powerful of irritants, the Introduction to the New Cambridge edition of *The Winter's Tale*, I gratefully record my debt.

For the explanation of abbreviated references, see 'Abbreviations' below (p. xiii).

ends or signs of hurried composition or alteration (J. H. P. Pafford, pp. xxvi, 64, 160)—is of course true, as it is of the work of lesser men; but it may very well be doubted whether it is especially true of Shakespeare, or whether it is truer of his Romances than of his earlier plays. In looking into Shakespeare's manipulation of the sources of *Cymbeline* Kenneth Muir found that he had taken 'infinite pains' with it (p. 232); and the present study points to much the same conclusion regarding the choice and disposition of the materials of *The Winter's Tale*.

Throughout the work I have kept a close eye on Greene's *Pandosto*, the principal source.[1] Taking 'the poetic reality alone' as the object of his Shakespearean criticism, Wilson Knight (p. 29) claimed to set his conclusions beyond the scope of 'the tracer of "sources", and the critic who must ever think in terms of Shakespeare's intentions'. The student who, like myself, takes a wider view of 'poetic reality' will think that Professor Knight draws too sharp a distinction between 'poetic and imaginative fact' and prosaic fact. It is well to be reminded of the labyrinthine nature of the creative process, but we must nevertheless insist on the relevance to that process of things of every day. We are, it seems to me, obliged to take source material into account, especially when, as in the case of *The Winter's Tale*, a single book stands out as having been the constant object of the writer's attention in the act of composition.[2] The comparison this affords may throw light on the creative process itself, and the details of the artist's selection and transformation may help to clarify his intentions.

In preparing this scene-by-scene commentary I have, I hope, approached the play with an open mind and, taking it as it comes, allowed it to assign its own emphases. Philip Edwards has usefully hinted at the dangers that attend 'critics who take us through one or more of the Romances, explaining as they go, like Bunyan's Interpreter, what it all really means'. Such a critic can be more faithful to his Interpretation than to the logically prior task of taking us through the detail of the work in hand. To do that is my main business in the following pages. The commentary offers an

---

[1] Hitherto the fullest studies of the relationship have been those of Lawlor and Pafford. See also Stanley Wells's useful comparison (*Later Shakespeare* pp. 64–70), which appeared after this book was finished.

[2] Lesser sources are discussed, e.g., by Muir (pp. 244–51) and Pafford (pp. xxxiii–xxxvii).

experience of the play as a transmutation of its primary source. I think of myself not as Interpreter but as Mr. Spectator the impartial observer seeking to record what is there for him to see.

The uniqueness of the last plays justifies this treatment. Whatever species we assign them to, each may almost equally well be regarded as an individual. The question of genre is generally important in establishing the ground of judgement; but where the object of criticism is presented in relative independence of critical context the appropriate criteria must be allowed to emerge from the work itself. The question of genre in this case is therefore relegated to an appendix; and as it is often considered in relation to the King's Servants' transfer to Blackfriars as their winter theatre I touch in the same appendix on that matter also.

The New Arden edition of *The Winter's Tale* is used for reference and quotation, and also the modern-spelling text of Robert Greene's *Pandosto, The Triumph of Time*, contained in the same volume. Where stage directions are mentioned they are those of the First Folio.

Abbreviations

The following abbreviations are used:

G. E. Bentley	'Shakespeare and the Blackfriars Theatre', *Shakespeare Survey* 1 (1948), pp. 38–50
S. L. Bethell	*The Winter's Tale: A Study* (1947)
J. R. Brown	John Russell Brown, *Shakespeare and his Comedies* (Second Edition 1962)
Chambers	E. K. Chambers, *The Elizabethan Stage*, 4 vols. (1923)
Nevill Coghill	'Six Points of Stage-Craft in *The Winter's Tale*', *Shakespeare Survey* 11 (1958), pp. 31–41
Coleridge	*Coleridge's Shakespearean Criticism*, ed. Thomas Middleton Raysor, 2 vols. (1930)
Quiller-Couch	*The Winter's Tale*, New Cambridge Shakespeare, ed. Sir Arthur Quiller-Couch and J. Dover Wilson (1931)
Cunningham	Peter Cunningham, *Extracts from the Accounts of the Revels at Court* (1842)
J. F. Danby	*Poets on Fortune's Hill* (1952)
Philip Edwards	'Shakespeare's Romances: 1900–1957', *Shakespeare Survey* 11 (1958), pp. 1–18
Inga-Stina Ewbank	'The Triumph of Time in *The Winter's Tale*', *A Review of English Literature*, V (1964), pp. 83–100
Northrop Frye	*A Natural Perspective* (1965)
Greene	Robert Greene, *Pandosto. The Triumph of Time*, in J. H. P. Pafford, pp. 184–225
F. D. Hoeniger	*Pericles*, (New) Arden Shakespeare, ed. F. D. Hoeniger (1963)

D. G. James   *Scepticism and Poetry* (1937)

Mrs. Jameson   *Characteristics of Women* (1832)

Frank Kermode *The Tempest*, (New) Arden Shakespeare, ed. Frank Kermode (1961)

Wilson Knight G. Wilson Knight, *The Crown of Life* (1948)

Later   *Later Shakespeare*, ed. John Russell Brown and
Shakespeare   Bernard Harris (Stratford-upon-Avon Studies 8, 1966)

John Lawlor   '*Pandosto* and the Nature of Dramatic Romance', *Philological Quarterly* 41 (1962), pp. 96–113

F. R. Leavis   'The Criticism of Shakespeare's Late Plays', *Scrutiny* X (1942), pp. 339–45

Clifford Leech *The John Fletcher Plays* (1962)

J. C. Maxwell *Cymbeline*, New Cambridge Shakespeare, ed. J. C. Maxwell (1960)

Kenneth Muir   *Shakespeare's Sources*, I (1957)

Allardyce Nicoll 'Tragical-comical-historical-pastoral', *Bulletin of the John Rylands Library* 43 (1960), pp. 70–87

J. M.   *Cymbeline*, (New) Arden Shakespeare, ed. J. M.
Nosworthy   Nosworthy (1955)

Stephen Orgel *The Jonsonian Masque* (1965)

J. H. P. Pafford *The Winter's Tale*, (New) Arden Shakespeare, ed. J. H. P. Pafford (1963)

Pandosto   As under Greene

R.E.S.   *Review of English Studies*

Ernest Schanzer 'The Structural Pattern of *The Winter's Tale*', *A Review of English Literature* V (1964), pp. 72–82

Shakespeare   *A Shakespeare Apocrypha*, ed. C. F. Tucker
Apocrypha   Brooke (1908)

Sidney   Sir Philip Sidney, *An Apologie for Poetrie*, in *Elizabethan Critical Essays*, ed. G. Gregory Smith (1904)

xiv

Irwin Smith	*Shakespeare's Blackfriars Playhouse* (1966)
S.S.	*Shakespeare Survey*
Derek Traversi	*An Approach to Shakespeare* (Second Edition, 1957)
Variorum	*The Works of Francis Beaumont and John Fletcher*, Variorum Edition, ed. A. H. Bullen, 4 vols. (1904–12)
Dover Wilson	*The Winter's Tale*, New Cambridge Shakespeare, ed. Sir Arthur Quiller-Couch and J. Dover Wilson (1931)

Prologue

I

Play titles can mean anything or nothing. 'We might as well have called it, God you good even', say the authors of *Eastward Ho*; yet even so, they add, their title is not without some point. How much point is there in *The Winter's Tale*? Is some quality of uniqueness suggested by *The*? Would the title not have been more suitable to *Pericles*, with its simple 'and then' narrative line, its scenes presented by a medieval story-teller? In that capacity Gower comes

> To sing a song that old was sung, . . .
> To glad your ear, and please your eyes.
> It hath been sung at festivals,
> On ember-eves and holy-ales;
> And lords and ladies in their lives
> Have read it for restoratives.

He introduces thus, to an audience 'born in these later times, / When wit's more ripe', a play in the manner of an antique tale. He does it with an air of great assurance and with the promise, it seems, of uncommon profit: 'The purchase is to make men glorious'.

The Winter's Tale in its title suggests another essay in that genre, but with no such ostentation, unless we find a hint of it in *The*. Rather it ostensibly implies, to use the phrasing of the play, that its 'verity . . . is in strong suspicion', that it will tediously 'have matter to rehearse, though credit be asleep and not an ear open'— even that it is something 'to be hooted at' (V, ii, 28, 62, V, iii, 116). The title may have the further modest intention of predisposing the playgoer to excuse, as in keeping with the matter of the play, anything in the means or method used (whether stage bear or moving statue, or time-gap of sixteen years) which may seem to him wildly at variance with dramatic propriety. Lyly proclaims just such implications when in *Endymion, The Man in the Moon* he devotes the whole prologue to glossing the title of the play:

Most high and happy Princess, we must tell you a tale of the Man in the Moon, which, if it seem ridiculous for the method, or super-fluous for the matter, or for the means incredible, for three faults we can make but one excuse: it is a tale of the Man in the Moon.

It was forbidden in old time to dispute of Chimæra because it was a fiction: we hope in our times none will apply pastimes, because they are fancies; for there liveth none under the sun that knows what to make of the Man in the Moon. We present neither comedy, nor tragedy, nor story, nor anything but that whosoever heareth may say this: Why, here is a tale of the Man in the Moon.

In this way the author leaves it open to the audience to receive his play as nothing more than light and fanciful entertainment; but by seeming to disclaim contemporary application he puts it in their minds to look for a sophisticated interpretation as well. Likewise Shakespeare, forestalling criticism by offering his work as a mere winter's tale, may suggest at the same time that it can profitably be approached with other expectations too.

A Midsummer Night's Dream is a parallel case, its title ostensibly implying a 'weak and idle theme, / No more yielding but a dream', and thereby hinting perhaps at a grace beyond the reach of reason. Commenting on the action of the play, the official touchstone, the rational and princely Theseus, says that he 'never may believe / These antique fables, nor these fairy toys'; but Hippolyta, more imaginative, is given the last word:

> But all the story of the night told over,
> And all their minds transfigur'd so together,
> More witnesseth than fancy's images
> And grows to something of great constancy;
> But, howsoever, strange and admirable.

These two plays, *A Midsummer's Night's Dream* and *The Winter's Tale*, combine courtly and popular elements in a setting of courtly or pastoral romance. One is a product of Shakespeare's professional midsummer, the other of the winter of his career. Between the two there lies a gap of fifteen or sixteen years. Perhaps Shakespeare, noting all this, saw with a smile a special appropriateness in his choice of title for *The Winter's Tale*, in pointing back by contrast to what in some ways is a companion piece. Though the mood of its transformation scenes—Leontes' possession, Hermione's reanimation—is very different from that of Bottom's translation or the transfiguring of the lovers' minds, both plays have their eye on the *Metamorphoses*. If Shakespeare goes to Ovid for the tragic story of Pyramus and Thisbe to turn it to riotous laughter, he finds in Ovid also Pygmalion's image, the prototype of love's power to give life to the inanimate. But the love-juice and the ass's head are the paraphernalia of fairy magic. The hate-juice (as we may call it) that so suddenly transforms Leontes, and the consequent petrifaction of Hermione, show the far more malign power of human magic in one of its aspects. This can wreak irrevocable destruction. Happily human magic has another aspect also, however, which can do much to heal, recover and renew; and through the exercise of this recreative magic husband and wife are finally restored to one another. We are reminded of *Pericles*, where Marina comes bringing 'sacred physic' to her father, and he thinks she may be a fairy or a dream; but she is flesh and blood, and being of extreme virtue she seems to possess recreative power, so that Pericles can call her 'Thou that beget'st him that did thee beget' (*Per.* V, i, 74, 155, 163, 197).

That quality of strangeness and wonder, a quality of 'great constancy' which Hippolyta recognizes in the world of imagination, the Romances can transfer to the world of ordinary life at extraordinary moments. It is deeply present in *The Winter's Tale*. The touchstone here is Paulina, a counterpart not of Theseus but of Hippolyta, ready in spite of reason to believe what transcends reason. Indeed she sets her hope and trust in it. She gains no supernatural power through study, has no Ariel at her command. Her magic is human magic, her power personal: the directing, conserving force of character, and a strange, intuitive knowledge of when "'Tis time' for 'dear life' to 'redeem' from death.

II

In his well-known paper on 'The Criticism of Shakespeare's Late Plays', F. R. Leavis drew attention to the differences that distinguish these plays one from another. We do well to remember that caveat; it provides justification for the present study, which deals with one of them in virtual isolation from the rest; and I return to it later in an appendix. For the present, however, I am concerned rather with their affinities. The Romances are curiously interrelated.

One may have been germinating in Shakespeare's mind while he was writing another.[1] Amongst their similarities in plot, theme, mood and character none is more notable, perhaps, than the occurrence in all four of the loss and reunion of members of the same family, sometimes as though from death itself. Indeed D. G. James (pp. 231, 233) has thought that in these plays 'the coming to life of the "dead"' is used to excess, with consequent weakening of force and importance. He lists eight cases. Thaisa alone, he says, 'is literally recovered from death'; the rest, 'Marina, the sons of Cymbeline, Posthumus, Imogen, Perdita, Hermione, Ferdinand, all reappear, as if, to those who thought them dead, from death to life'. But that is to reckon without the audience. In five of those instances there has been for the audience no question of death: the characters concerned are 'missing, presumed dead' by other characters on the stage, but not by the spectator, who knows the facts. The remaining three, Thaisa, Imogen and Hermione, have all seemed dead and have all gone through a form of burial. Thaisa, however, is known to be alive

---

[1] *Pericles* sounds the keynote of the group. After its completion Shakespeare's reading appears to have included materials for use in both *Cymbeline* and *The Winter's Tale*; and *The Tempest* was probably in prospect while *The Winter's Tale* was being prepared. In going over the story of Fawnia in Greene's *Pandosto* Shakespeare was evidently reminded of the story of Spenser's Pastorella (*F.Q.* VI, ixff.). We see evidence of this not only in *The Winter's Tale* but also in the name of Alonso's daughter Claribel in *The Tempest*, and possibly in the account of the mole on Imogen's breast in *Cymbeline*, which (unlike Boccaccio) Shakespeare describes as resembling a flower, which is how Spenser describes Pastorella's mole. Again, after reading *The Rare Triumphs of Love and Fortune* with *Cymbeline* in view, Shakespeare took the name of its hero Hermione and gave it to the heroine of *The Winter's Tale*; and from another source for *Cymbeline*, Boccaccio's *Decameron*, he derived the punishment of flaying alive, anointing with honey, etc., with which, with delightful extravagance, Autolycus threatens the Clown in the later play. The plot of *The Tempest* contains touches from *Love and Fortune* (Kermode, p. lix); Propsero's speech 'Ye elves of hills, brooks, standing lakes and groves' (*Temp.* V, i, 33) is closely modelled on one of the enchantress Medea's in Ovid's *Metamorphoses* (VII, 197–219), a work which Shakespeare had been recalling once again while engaged on *The Winter's Tale*; and the boat in which Prospero and Miranda are put to sea resembles that in which the infant Fawnia is cast out in *Pandosto*, 'having neither sail nor rudder to guide it'. What is more, Shakespeare is probably thinking of that same boat in Greene's romance—the source for *The Winter's Tale*—when he makes Pisanio observe in *Cymbeline* (IV, iii, 46), 'Fortune brings in some boats that are not steer'd'.

4

by the wonderful doctor Cerimon, and by the audience who have seen him revive her out of an advanced coma, and tell her where to live in seclusion. That Imogen is alive is known only to the audience: they see her wake from the effects of a drug which for a time has stopped the bodily functions, and they see her continuing to take part in the action under an assumed name. That Hermione is alive is known, it seems, to no one. She is dead: this is asserted by the most reliable witness in the play and is a truth accepted by everybody else until within fifty lines of the end. The happy reunions of long lost parents and children in these plays are all in varying degrees occasions of wonder to the persons concerned. The return of Hermione, however, which takes the audience also by surprise, is beyond question the most impressive and exciting case of all.

III

The structure of *The Winter's Tale* closely follows the arrangement of the material in *Pandosto*, but invests it with organic character.[1] In *Pandosto* the action is capricious, subject to the whims of Fortune. Envious of the 'happy success' of Pandosto, Bellaria and Garinter (Leontes, Hermione and Mamillius), Fortune in the first part of the tale,

> willing to show some sign of her unconstancy, turned her wheel, and darkened their bright sun of prosperity with the misty clouds of mishap and misery. (p. 185)

This part ends with the sudden death of Bellaria, out of grief for the equally sudden death of Garinter at the moment when, the oracle having been read, the king repents and all seems well. The second part passes to new characters, a new setting and new interests, but first to the infant Fawnia, who in the first part had been committed to the mercy of the waves. Now

> Fortune minding to be wanton, willing to show that as she hath wrinkles on her brows so she hath dimples in her cheeks, thought after so many sour looks to lend a feigned smile, and after a puffing storm to bring a pretty calm. (p. 199)

[1] Ernest Schanzer is overlooking *Pandosto* for the moment when he says (p. 73) that *Pericles* 'provided the structural model' of *The Winter's Tale*.

So the child is found and preserved by an old shepherd; and sixteen years pass rapidly, showing the stages of her growth. The love of Dorastus and Fawnia (Florizel and Perdita), whose story receives the chief emphasis in Greene's romance, is introduced with a further statement of Fortune's vagaries. She

> began now to turn her back and show a louring countenance, intending as she had given Fawnia a slender check, so she would give her a harder mate. (p. 202)

Wishing to marry, and thinking to escape the certain disapproval of Egistus (Polixenes) by sailing to Italy, they are drawn by fortune to the port of 'the chief city of Bohemia where Pandosto kept his court'. Here, though the fact is not explicitly stated, we enter upon a third part, with the return of Pandosto to the action. He makes advances to his unknown daughter which she firmly rejects. Her identity is revealed and Egistus, 'hearing this comical event, rejoiced greatly at his son's good hap', and hastened the marriage. After that, Pandosto 'fell into a melancholy fit, and to close up the comedy with a tragical stratagem, he slew himself'. Thus in Greene's hands, the story is quite disconnected, and the fulfilment of the oracle in the finding of Fawnia, far from being turned to account, is not even brought to notice.

The great changes that Shakespeare makes in the plot are, as everyone knows, to keep Leontes alive and to restore Hermione. More than that: he links Hermione's return with Perdita's discovery, making the hope that Perdita will be found the reason for her mother's preservation. This gives the play coherence. The restoration of Hermione is its strength, the point upon which all else in the play converges. It is essentially a sudden and theatrical event; and being the end and object of the whole may be expected to influence the earlier treatment of character and incident, so that its suddenness may, without losing force or prominence, accord with the prevailing tone.

IV

The last scene crowns the play, but in doing so it appears to break a generally accepted rule of dramatic construction. 'You must *never* keep a secret from your audience'. This was Yeats's advice to young playwrights, as reported by Frank O'Connor in developing the point.[1] 'At any given moment', O'Connor explained, 'the audience must be in full possession of the facts'. 'Obviously, knowledge that isn't shared, so far as the theatre is concerned, isn't knowledge at all'. The playwright knows that 'drama begins at the precise moment when he allows the audience to share in a knowledge which he withholds from one or more of the characters'. This is not true of every type of drama but it is of most drama that matters, and, what is to our present purpose, it is true of Shakespeare, except, it would seem, in *The Winter's Tale*. *Twelfth Night* provides a convenient illustration. In the opening scenes the amatory inclinations of the characters are arranged in a circle which it seems impossible to square to the satisfaction of all parties:

The problem is clearly stated at an early point in the play:

> How will this fadge? My master loves her dearly;
> And I, poor monster, fond as much on him;
> And she, mistaken, seems to dote on me.
> What will become of this? etc.   (II, ii, 34)

The dénouement consists in providing Viola with a twin brother who returns Olivia's love, whereupon the changeable Orsino responds to Viola's, thus squaring the circle:

But—and this is the point of the illustration—in II, i, the scene

[1] Frank O'Connor, 'The art of the Theatre', *The Bell*, vol. 9, No. 6 (March 1945), pp. 494ff. See also William Archer, *Play-Making* (1912) pp. 232 ff.

before Viola sums up the problem, the twin brother is brought upon the stage, showing his resemblance in feature and costume to his sister, and suggesting that since he is by no means dead, as she believes, something amusing and unexpected may come of the situation. Thus the spectator is put in possession of the full facts before the problem is stated: nothing is withheld from him as it is from the characters on the stage, and he is therefore able to enjoy the ensuing mistakes and cross-purposes as mistakes and cross-purposes.

The Winter's Tale seems entirely at variance with that. In the central scene Hermione is given out to be dead, and the report is confirmed by much corroboratory detail. No hint to the contrary is given at the time. Yet at the end she stands as a statue supposedly the work of a celebrated artist, and comes down alive to her husband's arms. And this is as much a surprise to the spectator (or almost as much) as it is to the characters on the stage.

Only a very ingenuous playgoer can accept without question that a woman will acquiesce in a pious fraud for sixteen years, living in seclusion within easy walking distance of her husband while he believes her dead, that at the end of that time she will allow herself to be put standing like a statue until told to move, and that till then she will remain unresponsive to the sight of her husband and of the daughter whom she has not seen since she gave her birth. Obviously such a scene can be accepted only on the level of fantasy not reason, on a level of apprehension which is not conditioned absolutely by the causal relations of everyday experience, and which admits suspension of disbelief for the moment that she who was dead is now restored to life.

In that mood of poetic faith we can freely admit that Shakespeare plays no trick at all in vehemently insisting in mid-play that Hermione is dead. At that time it is true: Hermione is dead, dead to Leontes. Later the truth changes and we are told of it the moment it changes. We are not kept in the dark regarding any essential fact. The spiritual estrangement of Hermione and Leontes was as absolute as if they had been separated by death. The possibility that they could be reunited was as remote as that of resurrection from the dead. The last scene, in appearing to present just that, *in effigie*—a resurrection from the dead, a turning of stone to flesh—represents the miraculous power of the human spirit, rightly directed, to achieve the impossible.

8

Act One   Scene One

The Winter's Tale unfolds its own story. Unlike *Cymbeline* and *The Tempest*, which embrace a long train of events lying in the past, it does not require an early scene of recapitulation. Yet it does not start with Leontes and Polixenes, but with an unassuming little scene between two gentlemen representing the two kingdoms, and relieving the kings of the need to create their own atmosphere *ab initio* in the next scene.

The tone is at once courtly and intimate, their mood one of unmixed satisfaction. The royal visit is in progress, and

> Sicilia cannot show himself over-kind to Bohemia. They were trained together in their childhoods, and there rooted betwixt them then such an affection which cannot choose but branch now. . . . [Mamillius] is a gallant child; one that, indeed, physics the subject, makes old hearts fresh.   (21, 37)

It is a rosy picture. Too good to be true, we may think; and looking back we can see striking ironies in the detail of the scene.[1] But we must not do so without seeing the countervailing irony as well, that in the normal world of this play goodness *is* truth, that Camillo and Archidamus represent what is the common courtly standpoint throughout the action. The immediate function of the scene is to present, in a dialect indicative of a courtly and pastoral play, a

---

[1] 1. 'If you shall chance, Camillo, to visit Bohemia . . .' (1). Camillo flees for his life to Bohemia at the end of the next scene.

2. 'I think, this coming summer, the King of Sicilia means to pay Bohemia the visitation which he justly owes him' (5). Leontes pays Polixenes no such visit in the course of the play, which, so far as Leontes is concerned, passes, one might say, in unbroken 'winter / In storm perpetual'.

3. 'I think there is not in the world either malice or matter to alter it' (33). There is not now, but in the very next scene there will be such malice, and in Leontes himself, self-engendered.

4. 'If the king had no son . . .' (44): an unthinkable hypothesis. But, in consequence of the king's 'malice', his son does die.

state of civilized normality. This serves as a background to the coming bestial abnormality.

Derek Traversi (p. 262) detects ambiguity in Camillo's statement that the kings' friendship 'cannot choose but branch', and interprets it as suggesting that 'though rooted and natural in its origins' their friendship 'bears within itself the cause of future disunion'. That suggestion is quite out of keeping with Camillo's cheerful mood: if he were intended to imply the possibility of future dissention he would be far from happy about it. A meaning for his words consistent with his optimistic frame of mind would be this: that the kings were brought up together like plants trained on a wall, between which was rooted the plant of affection; as a result of the nurture given then, this plant cannot choose but branch rightly now, holding the two kings together.

Later images of Camillo's tend to confirm this reading:

> they have seemed to be together, though absent; shook hands, as over a vast; and embraced, as it were, from the ends of opposed winds.[1] (28)

It seems a mistake, therefore, to look for ambiguity in Camillo's speeches. It is Leontes who in his abnormality will deal in ambiguities. Camillo and Archidamus are clear and direct in their outlook: it is the healthy, straightforward thing for a root to give a branch: 'no root, no branch' is a proverb. They represent normality in a civilized world, a world in which nature is not given the choice of whether to 'branch' or not: it cannot choose: it is

---

[1] The basic thought is Greene's 'neither tract of time nor distance of place could diminish their former friendship' (p. 185). Mr. Traversi sees sinister implications in 'opposed winds', but he neglects the overriding force of 'together', 'shook hands' and 'embraced'. The conception contained in the passage, of the spiritual union of friends, is in accord with the doctrine of the corporate unity of the family prominent in Shakespeare's later plays:

> Is it not as this mouth should tear this hand
> For lifting food to't? (*K.L.* III, iv, 15)

> She that herself will sliver and disbranch
> From her material sap, perforce must wither,
> And come to deadly use. (*K.L.* IV, ii, 34)

> . . . when from a stately cedar shall be lopped branches, which, being dead many years, shall after revive, be jointed to the old stock, and freshly grow, then shall Posthumus end his miseries. (*Cym.* V, iv, 140)

trained. There is no sign that the kings' friendship 'bears within itself the cause of future disunion'.[1]

That is the supreme irony: there is nothing inherent in the situation, as it has been presented to us, to show that abnormality may intrude in spite of training. Hermione has not been mentioned. Without her, so far as the play's postulates go, everything in the Garden of Sicilia would have remained idyllic.

With an exchange of jests to set off the regal stateliness of the principal characters' entrance the preliminaries are concluded.

Scene Two

I

Nevill Coghill interestingly points a contrast between the opening scenes of this play and of other plays of Shakespeare's. In *King Lear* and *Antony and Cleopatra*, he says, we are prepared for what we are about to see ('technique of gratifying expectation raised')—in *The Winter's Tale* for what we are about not to see ('technique of prepared surprise'). This sharp distinction is, however, seldom found, I believe, outside pure comedy. In all three of the plays in question we see both what we are led to expect and what we are not led to expect: Cornwall, Albany, and the division of Lear's kingdom, but also Cordelia and a trial of affection; Antony a strumpet's fool, but also magnificent folly, nobleness in ignobility;

---

[1] The search for double meanings in this initial scene represents the extreme of literary as distinct from dramatic interpretation of drama. M. M. Mahood (pp. 147f.) interprets 'trained' as I do, but like Derek Traversi weights other words in the scene with secondary meanings. Thus, when Archidamus in the first sentence of the play speaks of 'great difference between our Bohemia and your Sicilia', 'difference' for her means not only dissimilarity but 'contention', as 'we shall soon discover', and the names of the countries stand eponymously for the kings, as a later passage indicates. In this way, she claims, undertones are set up which help to 'prepare us for the estrangement of the kings'. However it may be in the study, where we may look back and compare, in the theatre we cannot be expected to take this first speech at anything but its face value. That is how Camillo takes it, and Archidamus concurs. It *is* what Professor Mahood says it only *seems* to be—explanatory chat. It would be a poor playwright who would start his play with double meanings before even a single meaning had been imparted.

the kingly 'brothers', but also Hermione—an idyllic state, but also a Fall.

She enters on her husband's arm, and is soon known to be the Queen of Sicilia, for the other king identifies himself at once by saying that he must now return home. This intention is a New Fact of which we received no warning in the first scene, and which, thus abruptly brought to our attention, we may expect to be developed, perhaps in connexion with that accompanying New Fact, Hermione.

Compared with II, i, where Leontes is to make an exhibition of himself, this scene is a relatively private one. The court stand aloof.[1] Yet though it is an intimate scene between friends, the friends are kings of romance, making their first appearance in the play, and their looks, bearing and speech must proclaim their station. They call one another brother; but they use the formal language of regal dignity.

Polixenes' elaborate opening speech, starting, 'Nine changes of the watery star hath been / The shepherd's note . . .', arouses the expectation, perhaps, of a play in a courtly pastoral mode, and transparently conceals amid the flowers of pastoral rhetoric what will be a serpent of suspicion to some members of the audience: his visit has lasted for nine months. If Sicilia is brief in comparison with Bohemia's elaborate courtesy, that is rather to be expected in the circumstances, and has been adumbrated at the prose level of the scene before by the contrasting attitudes of Archidamus the guest, extravagant and profuse in gratitude, and Camillo who, playing the deprecating host, can be much blunter ('You pay a great deal too dear for what's given freely').

II

It has been made a question whether Shakespeare intends Leontes to be shown as jealous from the beginning of the scene or as growing jealous before our eyes. Frank Kermode thinks that

[1] The stage direction says 'Enter Leontes, Hermione, Mamillius, Polixenes, Camillo'. As we learn from ll. 217–30, however, other courtiers besides Camillo are present as silent witnesses of Polixenes' change of mind at the queen's entreaty. They remain apart: even Camillo is quite unaware of Leontes' jealousy when he is called forward at l. 209 (or is called upon to re-enter, having exited with the other lords at l. 185?).

> Perhaps [Shakespeare] did not care; his purpose is to show peace and
> courtesy destroyed by a storm of diseased passion comparable with
> the Fall, a betrayal like that of Judas.[1]

As regards the dramatist's immediate purpose, that is well said,
but in regard to his workmanship Shakespeare was much more
careful than Professor Kermode's words would seem to suggest.[2]
And then there is Shakespeare's ultimate purpose to bear in mind:
peace and courtesy, though destroyed, are to return, to rise from
their own ruin. Is it not dramatically essential that we should see
Leontes in his true likeness before he is distorted, so that when he
comes to himself, purged, we may recognize him? If he is to be
saved, he must be seen to be worth saving. Surely, to look no
further than the present scene in theatrical performance (which,
we must agree, is the true test), the filth which he pours out in
the middle of it demands a gracious opening for him in contrast, so
that the scene may be given light and shade. With what other view
of the scene can one reconcile Hermione's expression of love for
her husband (42) and his for her (88)? Not, certainly, with 'the
livid face of Leontes' which Dover Wilson sees in the background
during the following much-quoted dialogue, making the passage,
he thinks, 'dramatically a masterpiece of irony':[3]

Hermione	Not your gaoler then,
	But your kind hostess. Come, I'll question you
	Of my lord's tricks, and yours, when you were boys.
	You were pretty lordings then?
Polixenes	We were, fair queen,
	Two lads that thought there was no more behind,
	But such a day to-morrow as to-day,
	And to be boy eternal.
Hermione	Was not my lord
	The verier wag o' th' two?
Polixenes	We were as twinn'd lambs that did frisk i' th' sun,
	And bleat the one at th' other: what we chang'd
	Was innocence for innocence: we knew not

[1] *Shakespeare, the Writer and his Work* (1964), ed. Bonamy Dobrée, pp. 393–4.

[2] See Appendix I A.

[3] Dover Wilson (pp. 131, 133) believes that 'the actor who plays Leontes should display signs of jealousy from the very outset and make it clear, as he easily may, that the business of asking Polixenes to stay longer is merely the device of jealousy seeking proof'.

> The doctrine of ill-doing, [no,] nor dream'd
> That any did. Had we pursu'd that life,
> And our weak spirits ne'er been higher rear'd
> With stronger blood, we should have answer'd heaven
> Boldly 'not guilty', the imposition clear'd
> Hereditary ours. (59)

Thus to recall in pastoral terms the contrast of childhood innocence and adult perversity when (though no one can know it) Leontes' fall is immanent may indeed be called a masterpiece of irony, even without the addition of a background. But, as it happens, there is a background, or so I believe, and a highly appropriate one: not Leontes' livid face, but Leontes playing happily with his son.[1]

Polixenes has announced his departure. Leontes has entreated him to stay longer, and, not succeeding, has drawn his wife into the conversation, enlisting her help. She starts well, as Leontes notes with satisfaction—'Well said, Hermione' (33)—and then for fifty lines there is no further word from him. What is he doing? He cannot be standing by or he would be included in the conversation. He cannot be just having an aimless word with Camillo or another courtier. It must be that he is intended to play with Mamillius, the only other member of the royal party, who if he were not drawn into the action at this point would be left unoccupied for more than half the time he is on the stage.[2]

This provides an interval during which Hermione and Polixenes can chat familiarly on, as in the passage just quoted, which continues:

Hermione   By this we gather
        You have tripp'd since.

Polixenes   O my most sacred lady,
        Temptations have since then been born to's: for

---

[1] If mathematical computation is to be trusted, Mamillius is five years old. Sixteen years later Leontes judges Florizel, Mamillius's almost exact contemporary, to be twenty-one (V, i, 117, 125).

[2] At what point does Leontes start playing with Mamillius? 'Well said, Hermione' could be equivalent to 'Well done—I'll leave you to it'. Hermione's mention of Polixenes' son, however (34), looks like a cue, putting Leontes in mind of Mamillius, who can conveniently bring himself to notice at this point. Leontes is still near by at l. 42, where Hermione speaks or calls out her endearment, as though approving and sharing his parental enjoyment.

In those unfledg'd days was my wife a girl;
Your precious self had then not cross'd the eyes
Of my young play-fellow.

Hermione   Grace to boot!
Of this make no conclusion, lest you say
Your queen and I are devils. Yet go on;
Th'offences we have made you do, we'll answer,
If you first sinn'd with us, and that with us
You did continue fault, and that you slipp'd not
With any but with us.

It is at this point that Leontes, having abandoned his interlude with the child, comes forward to ask, 'Is he won yet?' There can be no reasonable doubt, as Dover Wilson says, that Shakespeare intended Leontes to be seen as overhearing Hermione's last words, and that he wrote them as he did so that Leontes could be seen as misinterpreting them. Surprise and mystification are all that the actor need show ('What an odd thing to say. What can she be talking about?'). These together with resentment ('At my request she would not',87) are enough in the shorthand of stage psychology to constitute the seeds of jealousy. Here presumably is the answer to Polixenes' later question, 'How should this grow?' (431).

III

Nevill Coghill is on Dover Wilson's side in this debate.[1] The opening of the scene, he says, presents us with a calculated surprise. Instead of a pair of happy and affectionate friends we see the two

[1] So is Kenneth Muir (pp. 240–1):
Partly to save time, and partly to leave no doubt in the minds of the audience of Hermione's innocence, [Shakespeare] begins the play with Leontes already jealous; and he makes Hermione press Polixenes to stay in order to test his suspicions. This, at least, seems to be the most satisfactory way of playing the first scene.
Ernest Schanzer, however (p. 76), finds the notion 'quite unacceptable':
The idea that Leontes dissembles during the first part of the scene, merely acting the rôle of loving friend and husband, goes clear contrary to Shakespeare's evident intention of establishing in our minds the Paradise which Leontes loses through his insane delusion.

kings entering separately, Leontes wearing 'a look of barely controlled hostility that may at any moment blacken into a thundercloud'. Polixenes, he believes, addresses the end of his speech of thanks to Hermione, paying her compliment, standing beside her, perhaps upon his arm? She is, he says, visibly pregnant,[1] 'for a day later we hear of it'. This is 'grasped by the audience at her first entry, because they can see it is so; they hear the visiting king say he has been there nine months; who can fail to wonder whether the man so amicably addressing this expectant mother may not be the father of the child?' Clues to Leontes' attitude, Professor Coghill continues, are to be found in the dialogue. His taste for equivocation is evident from the start. 'Stay your thanks awhile; / And pay them when you part' is an ominous expression, for as Dover Wilson showed, 'praise in departing' is a proverb meaning 'wait till the end before praising'. In 'Tongue-tied our queen? speak you', '"Our queen" are cold vocables for married love, and "tongue-tied" is a familiar epithet for guilt'. 'It is clear', Professor Coghill concludes, that Leontes 'has long since been jealous and is angling now (as he admits later) . . . to catch Polixenes in the trap of the invitation to prolong his stay'.

The main answer to this case lies in a cardinal principle of Shakespearean interpretation—that a dramatic fact becomes a dramatic fact only when the audience learns of it, not before. Leontes says he is 'angling now' at l. 180. That is presumptive evidence that he is not angling before that. Hermione's pregnancy is first mentioned in the second act. It is not a factor in the present situation.

Shakespeare is faced with a delicate task in this scene. He must make plain that the relations of Hermione and Polixenes are altogether beyond reproach and at the same time give some

[1] R. G. Hunter (*Shakespeare and the Comedy of Forgiveness* (1965), 198) also writes of 'the pregnant Hermione of Act One', and Derek Traversi (p. 264), writing of Polixenes in I, ii, mentions 'Hermione, who is known to be with child'. Cf. J. R. Brown (p. 212): 'Hermione is in an advanced stage of pregnancy, but no reference is made to this obvious visual fact'. Cf. also John Lawlor (p. 107):

Shakespeare makes his Leontes the watchful and suspicious observer of a
Hermione visibly pregnant, exchanging pretty courtesies with Polixenes,
and Inga-Stina Ewbank (p. 88):

In *The Winter's Tale* Hermione's lying-in is immanent at the outset of the
play (Polixenes has been in Sicilia for 'nine changes of the watery star').

colour to Leontes' insane suspicions.[1] That is why he does not bring Hermione's pregnancy to light here. Only Leontes is to have suspicions, and they are to be completely groundless. To let us know that she is expecting a baby would in that context be misleading or disconcerting to an audience. It would also be embarrassing to the dramatist, for he could hardly fail to let Leontes use the knowledge there and then as fuel for his own jealousy. Shakespeare will exploit the full dramatic potentialities of the situation in the next scene, making Leontes subject his wife to gross public indignity by scorning and pointing at her as big with a bastard; and he is not a man to steal his own thunder. Nor does Shakespeare use ambiguous and tasteless cushions to let the audience *see* that the queen is pregnant. His way is neater, and more orthodox. The queen's ladies, when it is dramatically pertinent, remark on her condition, and in accordance with dramatic convention we at once accept the fact, without demanding ocular proof.

Professor Coghill's other points may be dealt with more summarily:

1. In his first speech Polixenes is not 'amicably addressing this expectant mother'. Conceivably he throws out a little compliment to her (she is *not* upon his arm, however, for the audience must understand at once that she is Leontes' queen not Polixenes'); but the speech of thanks is made to his 'brother' not Hermione (4).

2. There is nothing ominous in Leontes' reply (9) to that speech. 'Praise in departing' is a proverbial expression; 'thanks in departing' is not.

[1] The discreet reference to nine months, half remembered by the audience in the next scene, may subtly help in this, for who but a madman would suppose that the suspected intrigue could date from the very beginning of Polixenes' visit? But this is a trifle. Shakespeare is working with broad strokes. Hermione's 'familiar courtesy' (Greene's expression) is misinterpreted as excessive familiarity by a man who takes leave of courtesy; her actions in the line of honour and duty become meaningless to one suddenly dead to these conceptions. As she tries unavailingly to explain to him later, speaking of Polixenes:

> I lov'd him as in honour he requir'd,
> With such a kind of love as might become
> A lady like me; with a love, even such,
> So, and no other, as yourself commanded:
> Which not to have done I think had been in me
> Both disobedience and ingratitude
> To you, and toward your friend.   (III, ii, 63)

See also Appendix I A.

3. 'Tongue-tied' is an epithet for many other conditions besides guilt. The expression 'Our queen' is not out of keeping with other modes of address in the scene (e.g. Hermione's two-fold 'sir' in reply), and indeed in that general context can be seen to betoken respect and admiration not coldness.

IV

The stages of Leontes' disorder are doubt, active suspicion, flaming jealousy. His pride is hurt when Hermione prevails upon his childhood friend after he has failed to win him over. How clearly this is the beginning of his unsettlement appears when he later calls Camillo to speak to him:

Leontes   Camillo, this great Sir will yet stay longer.
Camillo   You had much ado to make his anchor hold:
When you cast out, it still came home.
Leontes   Didst note it?
Camillo   He would not stay at your petitions; made
His business more material.
Leontes   Didst perceive it?
—They're here with me already; whispering, rounding
'Sicilia is a so-forth': 'tis far gone,
When I shall gust it last.—How cam't, Camillo,
That he did stay?
Camillo   At the good queen's entreaty.
Leontes   At the queen's be't: 'good' should be pertinent,
But so it is, it is not. . . .
Camillo   . . . I think most understand
Bohemia stays here longer.
Leontes   Ha?
Camillo   Stays here longer.
Leontes   Ay, but why?
Camillo   To satisfy your highness, and the entreaties
Of our most gracious mistress.
Leontes   Satisfy?
Th' entreaties of your mistress? Satisfy?
Let that suffice.   (211)

That is later on. The aside, 'At my request he would not', marks the point by which the seeds of mistrust have been sown.

The incident of asking Polixenes to stay longer is of Shakespeare's invention. It corresponds after a fashion to the trial of affection in *King Lear*, where a molehill becomes a mountain, and a happy formality occasions a long train of unhappiness and disaster. What Leontes does in the furtherance of friendship wrecks it; Hermione's wifely loyalty he takes as evidence of infidelity. Interpreted so, the situation is intensely dramatic. This quality is lost if one supposes that Leontes starts the scene already jealous, as a result of a hypothetical series of pre-play incidents which have aroused and fed hypothetical suspicions.

Polixenes' long visit has come to an end. It is but common courtesy for Leontes to ask him to stay longer, but not for him to press his friend further when he refuses—except for a specific reason, which, as Polixenes observes (21), Leontes does not offer. Leontes loves his friend to the point of selfishness. In the circumstances Polixenes might well gracefully agree to stay since he is the guest and his host makes such an issue of it; no point of principle is involved, no involuntary revulsion as in the case of Cordelia ('I cannot heave / My heart into my mouth'), no urgent call from home. He is being as stubborn as Leontes. But he reckons without Hermione. She who dutifully has not yet spoken is as dutifully uncompromising when she does speak, to make sure that her husband gets what he wants. The special consideration for his hostess which as a man of courtesy Polixenes is obliged to show Hermione is backed by the warm regard in which he holds her as a lady, and when with a woman's privilege she forsakes argument and uses cajolement and mock-tyranny ('My prisoner? or my guest?') he is forced to comply.

After letting us see that the shaft of jealousy has struck home, Leontes fights back his disquiet with loving thoughts:

Leontes	At my request he would not.
	Hermione, my dearest, thou never spok'st
	To better purpose.
Hermione	Never?
Leontes	Never but once. (87)

But as Hermione gaily prattles on, the 'melancholy passion' that Greene ascribes at this point to Pandosto has time to gain possession of Leontes, as would appear from the gloom that falls across his recollection of his courtship:

> Why, that was when
> Three crabbed months had sour'd themselves to death,
> Ere I could make thee open thy white hand,
> And clap thyself my love; then didst thou utter
> 'I am yours for ever'.   (101)

She, delighted at the opportunity to please her husband by paying his dear fried a little compliment, unwittingly speeds Leontes' downfall:

> Why lo you now; I have spoke to th' purpose twice:
> The one, for ever earn'd a royal husband;
> Th' other, for some while a friend.

The irony of the time references is terrible: her gains—whether eternal husband or short-term friend—are both to be snatched from her almost at once and seemingly for ever. But that can be appreciated only after witnessing the play. What is immediately to the purpose is that Hermione makes the speech holding out her hand to Polixenes (the white hand she opened to clap herself Leontes' love), and that a passage of apparently clear and open interpretation thus lends itself to distortion in Leontes' mind. His suspicion is now far advanced. He takes up Hermione's last word 'friend': it rankles: this is *his* friend, but events have just shown that Hermione has more influence over him than Leontes has:

> Too hot, too hot!
> To mingle friendship far, is mingling bloods.
> I have *tremor cordis* on me: my heart dances,
> But not for joy—not joy.

This stage in the growth of his disorder is given emphatic dramatic statement. We can see that the man is violently excited. He says that he feels physically disturbed, that this has happened to him suddenly. And the cause is something that we can see: Hermione has taken Polixenes by the hand.

He struggles to compose himself, deluding himself that he is capable of rational judgement:

> This entertainment
> May a free face put on, derive a liberty
> From heartiness, from bounty, fertile bosom,
> And well become the agent: 't may I grant—

but he automatically distorts the evidence:

> But to be paddling palms, and pinching fingers,
> As now they are, and making practis'd smiles
> As in a looking-glass, and then to sigh, as 'twere
> The mort o' th' deer—O, that is entertainment
> My bosom likes not, nor my brows.

We may note in passing that Leontes does not say 'This confirms what I have seen in the past' (as he would if he had started the scene a jealous man), but 'There they are. It is plain for all to see', which is dramatically far more effective, putting the audience in full possession of the facts, so that nothing may be taken on hearsay. This is 'causeless jealousy', as Greene calls it, 'notoriously motiveless', as Bethell puts it; yet when we see it acted out before us we can see how and why it happens.

The man is far gone: his suspicions reflect themselves in quibbles, seeing likeness where no likeness is. He is ready to suspect his wife of adultery (119, 137), generalizing about women's falsity (130). When Mamillius comes to have his nose wiped—a domestic, universalizing, touch—Leontes has to reassure himself that his son is legitimate (120–3, etc.). But while taking comfort in the reassurance—and indeed turning to the boy as a refuge (126, 137) from what he half-wishes not to see—his eyes are upon Hermione 'Still virginalling', as he puts it, upon Polixenes' palm; and his thoughts are on horns and unfaithfulness (123–5, 128, etc.). Finally he breaks down in incoherence;[1] the excitement of his heart has given place to the infection of his brains (110, 145). He is now distracted with jealousy, and the passage to this final stage in his derangement is again marked by the use of arresting movement on the stage. Leontes claps his hands to his head (146, cf. 149), and Polixenes and Hermione come hurrying

---

[1] J. H. P. Pafford (pp. 165ff.) has a valuable note on ll. 137–46. It is indeed possible ,with H. G. Goddard (*The Meaning of Shakespeare* (1951), 651) or Hallett Smith (*Shakespeare Quarterly*, XIV (1963), 163), to make sense of what Leontes is saying and to see him as examining the nature of his own rising distemper, even as it grows upon him. Shakespeare abhors a vacuum, and in framing the spectacle of Leontes' unsettlement in incoherent monologue he makes the incoherence at least somewhat informative to the audience. But incoherence it remains: as Pafford says, 'Leontes is tortured in mind and in speech and this clouded, bitter language also effectively illustrates his condition'.

forward ('What means Sicilia?' / 'He something seems unsettled'.).[1]

This brings Hermione and Polixenes back into the action after almost forty lines of soliloquy-material half-exchanged, by the dramatist's skilful contrivance, with the uncomprehending little boy. Leontes now pulls himself together, talking to compose himself, resuming the safe topic of his likeness to Mamillius. Then, somewhat composed, he asks his son, half in jest, half with cunning, 'Will you take eggs for money?' 'No, my lord, I'll fight', Mamillius replies; and Leontes approves, for he also will not be content with something worthless—a worthless wife—and he too will fight back. Fortified in spirit he turns to the enemy, Polixenes, whom he has not spoken to since he yielded to Hermione's persuasions, and treacherously calling him 'brother' asks with apparent affability, 'Are you so fond of our young prince, as we / Do seem to be of ours?' The gist of Polixenes' reply is that he 'with his varying childness cures in me / Thoughts that would thick my blood'. This comes somewhat near the bone. It has the effect of heaping damnation on Leontes, making him seem to fall through his own wilfulness. In his melancholy his blood is thick, stopping up the access and passage to remorse. The varying childness of Mamillius could cure this condition if Leontes would let it, but he will not: pity is the last thing he wants. Though playing the part of a friend he can respond only half-heartedly to Polixenes' warm praise of childhood and packs him off to the garden with Hermione, cunningly giving line so as to catch the fish while pretending love for them both (181, 176), observing, and when they pass from view, imagining, generalizing, filling his mind with foul thoughts. He takes perverted comfort in the reflection that in being a cuckold he is not unique (196, 190, 198), and ironically thinks of adultery in terms descriptive of his own disease of jealousy:

> Physic for't there's none:
> It is a bawdy planet, that will strike
> Where 'tis predominant. (200)

[1] They can see that he is mentally disturbed—'unsettled', holding 'a brow of much distraction'. Hermione thinks he may be angry ('Are you mov'd, my lord?') but it does not occur to her that he can be angry with her. In Greene Pandosto 'began to bear . . . a louring countenance to Bellaria', so that she wondered what she had done to 'offend her husband'. Shakespeare allows only this brief moment of concern for her husband to cloud Her-

He said he wanted to walk with Mamillius, but that was just an excuse to be alone. In fact he keeps him at a distance (187, 190); and when the boy insists on receiving attention by saying what he knows will please ('I am like you, you say' 208), Leontes answers half-abstractedly, and kindly but firmly sends him away.

Thus Mamillius is gradually withdrawn from the scene, in token of Leontes' increasing spiritual isolation. He has served the dramatist well, providing diversity of method and poignancy of tone. Speaking but four half-lines he has yet been Leontes' most constant companion, a gallant child 'of the greatest promise' setting off the ugliness of his father's transformation. He has stood as a symbol of Leontes' lost innocence, enduing the successive stages of his fall with a sense of 'the pity of it'. And as the object of his father's abiding love, his playful endearments, his yearning for comfort, Mamillius has saved Leontes in the eyes of the spectator, and ensured that he will not altogether lose our sympathy.[1]

V

The replacement on the stage of Mamillius by Camillo marks the culmination of Leontes' rational irrationality. He analyses the grounds of suspicion as what can be seen, heard (by rumour) and thought—that is, imagined (267). Now that Polixenes and Hermione are no longer present, and Camillo, he finds, has no rumours to report, Leontes draws freely on his imagination—not, as before, basing his fancies on what is in front of him. The devastating irony of Shakespeare's writing against Leontes is nowhere more evident than here:

[1] J. H. P. Pafford (p. lxxxii) rightly remarks that Mamillius 'helps to bring out the characters of Leontes and Hermione and to give a human, domestic atmosphere to the court: his open goodness acts as a foil to the introverted evil in Leontes and his charm and vitality add to those qualities in the total effect of the play'. He concludes, however: 'But whatever importance is attached to Mamillius it must be remembered that his episode follows fairly closely that of Garinter in *Pandosto*'. His comment appears therefore to overlook the part taken by Mamillius in the present scene, which has no counterpart in *Pandosto*.

mione's happiness in this scene. Leontes stands alone: none but he can entertain suspicions.

> Is whispering nothing?
> ... wishing clocks more swift?
> Hours, minutes? noon, midnight? and all eyes
> Blind with the pin and web, but theirs; theirs only
> That would unseen be wicked? is this nothing?
> Why then the world, and all that's in't is nothing,
> The covering sky is nothing, Bohemia nothing,
> My wife is nothing, nor nothing have these nothings,
> If this be nothing.   (284)

There is nothing so dangerous as the diseased mind (296) that thinks it can think rationally:

> Dost think I am so muddy, so unsettled,
> To appoint myself in this vexation; sully
> The purity and whiteness of my sheets, ...
> Without ripe moving to't? Would I do this?
> Could man so blench?   (325)

This is an excellent piece of dramatic economy. To us who have witnessed the growth of Leontes' jealousy, his argument seems the ultimate in self-delusion. But Camillo does not know what we know, and it is specious enough to convince him. This, then, is an appropriate point at which to end this phase of the scene, Leontes mistakenly thinking that he has got what he wants. He promises Camillo that he will seem friendly to his intended victim (350), but how little he has himself under control we learn a moment later. He and Polixenes meet at once off stage, and Leontes hurries contemptuously past his friend without a word (365, 372). This speeds the action forward. Polixenes can have no doubt concerning Leontes' intentions, having seen his change of face and manner ('I saw his heart in's face', 447), and hence can readily believe Camillo.

In *Pandosto* when Franion, Camillo's counterpart, tells Egistus that he has been ordered to murder him, Egistus strongly suspects his good faith. This is something of a narrative indiscretion, for it makes Egistus seem to share Pandosto's attitude of mind. Polixenes, on the other hand, quickly agrees with Camillo: this not only accelerates the transition but gives a clearer and stronger moral contrast. Only Leontes is suspicious, introverted, a man untrue to himself: 'You never spoke what did become you less', Camillo tells him (282). Polixenes is a man of honour (400, 407), like Camillo belonging to the free and open world of the first scene.

That world is now on the run, however, intent on saving its own skin, and there is nothing Shakespeare can do to make it appear noble in abandoning Hermione, for there is nothing noble it can do. The action of the play depends on her being left to face the music alone, and Polixenes must therefore be lowered in our esteem.[1] He is a secondary figure used by the dramatist as a sort of utility man—in the present scene to impress on us by his almost religious veneration (76, 417, 441) a right sense of Hermione's virtues, in the fourth act to represent, in contrast to the freedom and openness of youth, the duplicity and repressiveness of age. For him to lose face somewhat with the audience now, therefore, will sort well enough, perhaps, with his new *persona* in Act IV. But in view of his respect and admiration for Hermione we are bound to make excuses for him, and to remind ourselves that in flying for his life he does what we have blamed Leontes for not doing—he takes the advice of the wise Camillo.

VI

Like Polixenes, Camillo will be absent from the action for two whole acts; but on his return he will have a vital part to perform, and it is vital that we should get to know and value him now. He is a generation older, it seems, than Leontes and Polixenes (461). He is a man of honour, good, wise, reliable, a perfect counsellor. Speaking of the time before he lost his spiritual eye-sight Leontes says:

[1] He gives clear and convincing reasons for thinking Leontes deadly dangerous, and is frightened to death (451, 461); but this is far from justifying him as a man of honour in a high romance. Shakespeare's recreative imagination does not set itself to transform Egistus. The fine image 'Fear o'ershades me' (457) shows the *poet's* sensitive mind at work in reading *Pandosto*, but not the *dramatist's*. The expression takes its origin in Greene's statement of Egistus's fear of Franion:

Egistus had not fully heard Franion tell forth his tale, but a quaking fear possessed all his limbs, thinking that there was some treason wrought, and that Franion did but shadow his craft with these false colours (p. 189).

> I have trusted thee, Camillo,
> With all the nearest things to my heart, as well
> My chamber-counsels, wherein, priest-like, thou
> Hast cleans'd my bosom: I from thee departed
> Thy penitent reform'd. (235)

So when the queen is calumniated, Camillo springs at once to the defence of honour and virtue in her, and to the service of honour and virtue in the king, speaking out against him as he would strike out at another:

> I would not be a stander-by, to hear
> My sovereign mistress clouded so, without
> My present vengeance taken: 'shrew my heart,
> You never spoke what did become you less
> Than this; which to reiterate were sin
> As deep as that, though true. (279)

Priest-like he urges spiritual cure:

> Good my lord, be cur'd
> Of this diseas'd opinion, and betimes,
> For 'tis most dangerous. (296)

But being a wise man he knows when a cure is beyond him, and where prudent self-interest must be his only guide:

Camillo   You may as well
Forbid the sea for to obey the moon,
As or by oath remove or counsel shake
The fabric of his folly, whose foundation
Is pil'd upon his faith, and will continue
The standing of his body.
Polixenes   How should this grow?
Camillo   I know not: but I am sure 'tis safer to
Avoid what's grown than question how 'tis born. (426)

Camillo takes his place beside Cerimon, Pisanio and Gonzalo as a wise counsellor who interprets duty in the spirit rather than the letter. In refusing to obey a king who is in rebellion with himself (354) he averts disaster in the present scene. Loyalty to Sicilia is his rule of life (after sixteen years in Polixenes' service he will still speak of Leontes as 'my master') and faced with what seem unthinkable alternatives—to obey the king and do evil, or to disobey him and lose his place—he momentarily inclines to the

26

course of habit—to obey the king. But his fundamental soundness at once reasserts itself:

> If I could find example
> Of thousands that had struck anointed kings
> And flourish'd after, I'd not do't: but since
> Nor brass, nor stone, nor parchment bears not one,
> Let villainy itself forswear't. I must
> Forsake the court: to do't, or no, is certain
> To me a break-neck. (357)

Yet even at this lowest point in his fortunes, when he must abandon his king, his country, and the employment he has enjoyed for so long, the optimism he showed in the opening scene does not forsake him. 'Happy star reign now', he prays. It does. Polixenes enters; and this enables Camillo to do good both to another and to himself, a congenial conjunction of events which he afterwards effects again in returning to Sicilia.

Act Two   Scene One

I

Once again Mamillius appears as a background to Leontes' enormity. Indeed the idea of using him so in I, ii, grew out of his prospective use in this scene, which develops a passing reference in Greene's *Pandosto*. In Greene, when the guard came to take the queen to prison, 'they found her playing with her young son Garinter' (p. 190).

Shakespeare gives the incident variety and dramatic interest, combined with telling brevity. He places it in the forefront of our attention, starting the act with it: it gives contrast, showing the lighter, more domestic side of court life. He divides it between (1) the queen, who grows tired of playing with the boy; (2) her ladies joking with him, casually telling us of the queen's condition —perhaps their primary dramatic purpose—giving the play a snatch of feminine court gaiety; and (3) the queen again, now the mother figure, trying to get him to sit down quietly and tell her a winter's tale:

Hermione	Come sir, now
	I am for you again: 'pray you, sit by us,
	And tell's a tale. . . .
	Come on, sit down, come on, and do your best
	To fright me with your sprites: you're powerful at it.
Mamillius	There was a man—
Hermione	Nay, come sit down: then on.
Mamillius	Dwelt by a churchyard: I will tell it softly,
	Yond crickets shall not hear it.
Hermione	Come on then,
	And giv't me in mine ear. (21)

In this miniature scene Mamillius is the centre of attention, a major speaking part with nine brief speeches out of twenty-two, Hermione coming next with six. The queen 'rounds apace'; 'a

29

fine new prince' is on the way. Mamillius sits beside her as a manifestation of that normal, natural, positive process; and as their voices fade into the background Leontes enters, abnormal, unnatural, negative, disrupting the gentle quiet with crude violence:

Leontes	Give me the boy: I am glad you did not nurse him. . . .
Hermione	What is this, sport?
Leontes	Bear the boy hence, he shall not come about her,
	Away with him, and let her sport herself
	With that she's big with; for 'tis Polixenes
	Has made thee swell thus.

For mother and child there are no preliminaries, no warning even of Leontes' presence—just unexpected, brutal shock. For the audience, however, there is an informatory speech linking this scene with the last. For dramatic effect Shakespeare has inverted Greene's narrative order, setting the scene in the queen's apartments before giving the reason for her impending imprisonment. Hence Leontes' speech now. Polixenes and Camillo have got away. Hearing of this he has not, like Pandosto, sent the guard to apprehend his wife but has hotfoot come himself, even as he is receiving reports. All his suspicions, he believes, were fully justified; he has been outwitted; he is a pinched thing. Greene's conclusion, that his enemies being out of the way Pandosto 'determined to wreak all his wrath on poor Bellaria', is not expressed, but exemplified in action.

II

The passage of time up to this point in the play is a question which does not seem to have received attention.[1] The first two scenes are linked by the presence in both of Camillo and by his talk with Archidamus of the royal friends, who then appear in person. II, i, shows Leontes quickly apprised of the flight of Polixenes and Camillo which occurs at the end of the scene before. Thus it would seem that the action so far has been continuous except for one

[1] But Inga-Stina Ewbank (pp. 87f.) has pertinent comments on the 'unnatural haste' and 'frenzied hurry' of the thoughts and actions in the opening movements of the play.

short break. For Dover Wilson there is no more to be said: he omits '*Exeunt*' at the end of I, i, substituting '*they pass out of hearing*'; and at the head of Act II he inserts '*Some hours pass*'.

On the other hand one can make a case for a more leisurely passage of time. When Polixenes gives his speech of thanks saying that he is leaving on the following day (I, ii, 10), he appears to have already exceeded 'the gest / Prefix'd for's parting' (41) by two days (450). But the conversation of Camillo and Archidamus in I, i, is not that of two men about to part. Archidamus's mention of the 'occasion whereon my services are now on foot' seems rather to imply that the royal visit is still running its course. This suggests a gap of at least some days—more likely weeks— between the first two scenes. The gap could run into months. In I, i, Camillo thinks that Leontes will pay a return visit 'this coming summer' (5). The expression suits a winter rather than an autumn speech (the action of II, i, passes in winter, 25) but does not rule out the possibility of autumn.

But this is to miss the point in irrelevant particularity. Let us put the matter more pertinently. I, i, is a typical scene between the two men, elastic in time reference. As befits the relaxed and friendly mood, time does not matter. That scene contrasts sharply in this respect with Leontes' entrance hard upon the fugitives' flight (a definite point in time), just as Leontes' entrance on that occasion contrasts sharply with the intervening revelation of Hermione's pregnancy, which is a relaxed and happy scene, suggestive of the slow maturing of time not violent immediacy. In other words, the opening of the second act, with Hermione expecting to have her baby soon, leads us to suppose that some months have passed, and then, in keeping with the harsh and unnatural mood that is in the ascendant, we are abruptly and disconcertingly disabused.

III

In inverting Greene's narrative order Shakespeare brings Hermione's pregnancy to light before she goes to prison. This invests her and the opening of the act with a special tenderness, and enhances the enormity of Leontes' violence and cruelty, to which her confinement 'something before her time' (reported in the next scene) is directly attributable.

Hermione is now the centre of attention. Leontes holds her up to public calumniation, eyeing her, pointing her out, calling her filthy names, inviting the lords to scorn and mock at her as an adulteress. More, she is a traitor, he says, privy to the escape of Polixenes her paramour and Camillo their pander.

All this only helps to bring out her noble nature. Gentleness and calm are her ruling characteristics. She is not stung to vulgar reproach:

> *Leontes*　She's an adulteress.
> *Hermione*　　　　　　Should a villain say so
> 　　　　　　(The most replenish'd villain in the world)
> 　　　　　　He were as much more villain: you, my lord,
> 　　　　　　Do but mistake.　　　　　　　　　　　　　　　(78)

She has spirit, but it arms her for endurance not rebellion or display of injury. Though her grief is deep and burning, it is not in her nature to resort to tears; yet she does expect the lords to be charitable as well as judicious in their appraisal. The fulness of her grief is inclusive not self-centred: she sees at once the difference Leontes' accusation has made to him and to their relationship:

> 　　　　　　　　　　How will this grieve you,
> 　　When you shall come to clearer knowledge, that
> 　　You thus have publish'd me! Gentle my lord,
> 　　You scarce can right me throughly, then, to say
> 　　You did mistake.　　　　　　　　　　　　　　　　(96)

Leontes' long sorrows are implicit in the situation: and in mentioning that the action she now goes on is for her better grace Hermione may be thought to imply the hope that his sorrows too will work for his eventual spiritual betterment. That the heavens will 'look / With an aspect more favourable' (106), that Leontes will 'come to clearer knowledge', that she will 'come out' of prison (121)—of all this she is confident; but when? Time does not enter into her calculations.[1] In her composed and timeless contemplation of grief Shakespeare may have thought of her as the human embodiment of Patience on a monument, 'smiling /

---

[1] Johnson's definition of patience comes to mind—'The quality of expecting long without rage or discontent'.

Extremity out of act' (*Per.* V, i, 138). If so, of course, this thought is the origin of the statue scene.

Hermione's bearing resembles that of a saint and martyr. On account of that likeness her plight is not tragic. Her tragedy is resolved in religious certainty. To make this point clear we may call to mind Christ's last words on the cross as reported by the evangelists. Considered as a human utterance and interpreted as it stands 'My God, my God, why hast thou forsaken me?' is an expression of the deepest tragedy, for it implies a sense of failure and betrayal, the sudden loss of the ground of trust. 'Father, into thy hands I commend my spirit', on the other hand, and 'It is finished', convey complete attunement with the will of God the Father. Far from being a tragedy, the Cross is here the accomplishment of the final stage of a plan, after which will come the return of the Son to the Father's presence.

In Hermione's quiet confidence there is likewise no tragedy. She is certain of her own innocence, certain that affliction will be for her good, that Leontes will come to himself and that her own reputation will be cleared:

> Do not weep, good fools,
> There is no cause: when you shall know your mistress
> Hath deserv'd prison, then abound in tears
> As I come out: this action I now go on
> Is for my better grace. Adieu, my lord:
> I never wish'd to see you sorry; now
> I trust I shall. (118)

So Hermione goes to prison, completely mistress of the situation. Indeed in her easy composure she unintentionally makes Leontes look absurd, as he expostulates ineffectively, trying to seem in command:

Hermione   and so
      The king's will be perform'd.
Leontes   Shall I be heard?
Hermione   Who is't that goes with me? Beseech your highness,
      My women may be with me, for you see
      My plight requires it. . . .
            . . . My women, come: you have leave.
Leontes   Go, do our bidding: hence!

IV

Before proceeding it will be helpful to look more closely at the sequence of events in *Pandosto* covered from this point up to the middle of the play:

(1) The guard take Bellaria to prison, where after some time she finds herself quick with child.

(2) The gaoler, learning this, tells Pandosto.

(3) When the child is born Pandosto orders that it be burnt, but abates his cruelty somewhat in response to the nobles' intercession.

(4) At her first trial 'the noblemen which sate in judgement' seek to support Bellaria's claim to a fair trial, but Pandosto silences them. Bellaria, however, asks that the Oracle of Apollo be consulted; and this Pandosto cannot refuse.

(5) Six noblemen are sent to the Isle of Delphos and return with the Oracle's answer.

(6) At the second trial the oracle is read. Pandosto comes to his senses and makes public confession. Then Garinter is reported to have died, and in consequence Bellaria falls down dead.

These episodes in order—omitting (4)—form the basis of Shakespeare's five scenes from II, i, to III, ii. We note that Bellaria confronts Pandosto in (4) and (6), and that the nobles speak out on her behalf in (2) and (4). Shakespeare's omission of (4), therefore, the first trial scene, leaves him, according to Greene's pattern, with only one confrontation scene between Hermione and Leontes, (6), and one scene in which the lords support her cause. As for Hermione, she is a character to be used sparingly, not staled by repetition, but obviously she must be given one major scene between Act I and her trial. Hence, as we have seen, the raising of the present scene in importance and dramatic force by bringing Leontes into it.

As for the lords it is a different matter. A second scene of intercession (anticipating 'We all kneel') might take from the play not strengthen it. On the other hand it is part of Shakespeare's purpose to make it manifest that Leontes is alone in his evil; and if we can be constantly reminded of that, all to the good. Camillo has already played his part in that connexion. The decision to bring Leontes into the present scene can be extended to include his courtiers, to witness for the first time the king's transformation and to manifest a unanimous sense of outrage. By presenting Hermione's plight not merely as the occasion of pity as an automatic response but more as an object of deliberate compassion—of emotion rationally sanctioned—the danger of repetitive effect in the scene with the helpless baby (II, iii) can be obviated here:

> Good my lords,
> I am not prone to weeping, as our sex
> Commonly are; the want of which vain dew
> Perchance shall dry your pities: but I have
> That honourable grief lodg'd here which burns
> Worse than tears drown: beseech you all, my lords,
> With thoughts so qualified as your charities
> Shall best instruct you, measure me.   (107)

But between the two scenes there must be more than avoidance of overlap. There must be significant difference. In the first of Greene's corresponding incidents, (3) above, the noblemen become 'importunate upon' the king; in the second, (4), 'seeing the king in choler', they are 'all whist'. This is a useful distinction; but it is what immediately follows in (4) that is truly seminal:

> The noblemen . . . were all whist; but Bellaria, whose life then hung in the balance, fearing more perpetual infamy than momentary death, told the king if his fury might stand for a law that it were vain to have the jury yield their verdict; and therefore, she fell down upon her knees, and desired . . . that it would please his majesty to send . . . to inquire of the Oracle of Apollo. . . .

This first trial Shakespeare suppresses; but in this detail of it Bellaria plays the part which Shakespeare appropriates more forcefully to Paulina, not in proposing the consultation of the Oracle, but in standing up to the choleric king when all the lords are 'whist'. Instead of a chorus of noblemen all becoming 'importunate upon' the king, we have one character representing Importunity, an outspoken woman, like Bellaria in Greene's first trial scene exercising a woman's licence and having nothing to lose by speaking out. Introducing Paulina in II, ii, performing the function of Greene's gaoler in (2)—a comparative lull in the action—is one of those dexterous strokes that seem so inevitable that the skill of their placing passes almost unnoticed. The idea of creating this strong-minded woman to appear in that scene may well have suggested to Shakespeare the invention of a hen-pecked husband for her, to represent the contrary courtierly attitude of goodness and loyalty easily tongue-tied by authority. In this way the concrete demands of dramatic form are answered: if there is a chorus, there is a leader of the chorus; if a representative attitude is to be conveyed, it is best represented through a distinctive individual. The corollaries will be that the baby will be taken away in obedience to Leontes' commands not by guards or shipmen merely, as in Greene, or by a nameless, characterless First Lord, but by Antigonus, husband of Paulina—a good man but a subservient courtier, easily 'whist'—and that she, importunate, knowing her own mind—not one of the 'crickets' of the present scene—having already taken over the function of a nameless Gaoler in *Pandosto*, will by force of character direct Leontes and his affairs to a happy issue.

V

When Hermione departs, then, the lords break out against Leontes. Till she went she was unsupported, facing her husband's insane rage alone: speeches on her side had been forbidden (104). Now in spite of prohibition everyone speaks up for her. This is the scene where, Paulina not being yet, dramatically speaking, in existence (she has not so far been mentioned), the nobles can be made most 'importunate upon' the king. In the scene after next, where she does appear, they will easily be put to silence, setting off Paulina's vehement strength and certainty. Here it is Hermione's gentle strength and certainty that we are concerned with, and the lords are, at this dramatically fitting time, her strong and certain champions.

Outstanding among them is Antigonus, displaying what we can afterwards discern as the inner strength of a man who in his wife's presence is apparently weak. He is to be a good deal more voluble than all the rest put together: so Shakespeare starts with one of the others, beseeching Leontes to call the queen back. This gives Antigonus his springboard, and with a firmness and insight which forsake him somewhat after Paulina appears the old man at once points to the heart of the matter:

> Be certain what you do, sir, lest your justice
> Prove violence, in the which three great ones suffer,
> Yourself, your queen, your son.

That is an important reminder of the general issues involved; but the rest of the scene concerns itself with what is uppermost in the courtiers' minds, the defence of Hermione's honour. Antigonus having broken the ice another lord protests that he would lay down his life 'that the queen is spotless'; and Antigonus (brushing aside interjections from Leontes and a third lord eager to have his say) warmly takes up this theme, making it a deeply intimate concern. If Hermione is honour-flawed 'every inch of woman in the world, / Ay, every dram of woman's flesh is false', and he will confine his own wife like a promiscuous animal, geld his own daughters—'And I had rather glib myself, than they / Should not produce fair issue'. Leontes, managing to get a word in, develops the physical vein—in his high-handed and insensitive way pulling the old man's nose, and asserting that because Antigonus has not his experience of marital dishonour

> You smell this business with a sense as cold
> As is a dead man's nose. (151)

Stung by the indignity—smarting not only with physical pain but with the vulgar taunt that he is on the brink of the grave—Antigonus seizes on Leontes' images of skull and stench to expose the gross fantasy of the king's obsession and to show up by contrast the certainty of his own faith. Antigonus may be already half dead, he says, but if Leontes is right about Hermione and she is false, honour needs no grave, for no grain of it exists to sweeten the foul smell of this earth, the very muck-hill, as Malevole put it, on which the sublunary orbs cast their excrements:

> If it be so,
> We need no grave to bury honesty:
> There's not a grain of it the face to sweeten
> Of the whole dungy earth. (154)

VI

In *Pandosto* the queen's trial is suspended and resumed three weeks or so later, because Bellaria falls on her knees in the course of it and begs the king to send to the Oracle at the 'Isle of Delphos'. Shakespeare, as we have seen, saves himself an abortive trial, and we should have expected him to transfer Bellaria's request to the present scene. The decision to consult the Oracle is indeed announced here, but the king has made the decision of his own mere motion. This is not intended to stand to his credit, however, but rather with reiterated crime to heap on him more discredit. He has already dispatched his deputation to the Oracle: that is to say, he has forejudged the issue, for he can have done so only before he knew that his plan to poison Polixenes had miscarried.

Lest we should miss the point Shakespeare puts it in Leontes' own mouth. After his courtiers' plain-spoken and wise criticism (158, 170) the absolute monarch (161) has tried to appear fair and reasonable

> (For in an act of this importance, 'twere
> Most piteous to be wild),   (181)

open (in revealing what he has already done secretly), and submissive to the god

>   whose spiritual counsel had,
> Shall stop or spur me.

He has sought and received (from one lord) approbation. And then with crass ineptitude he reveals his true state of mind. He has sent to the Oracle from politic motives: he is not interested in divine guidance. With gross impiety he puts himself before the god:[1]

> Though I am satisfied, and need no more
> Than what I know, yet shall the Oracle
> Give rest to the minds of others, such as he [Antigonus],
> Whose ignorant credulity will not
> Come up to th' truth.   (189)

---

[1] Pandosto likewise, learning that the queen was with child, swore 'that she and the bastard brat she was big withal should die if the Gods themselves said no' (p. 192). This is the germ of Leontes' rejection of the oracle, Shakespeare's vital alteration of the plot.

That is the stuff of tragedy. To avoid that emphasis here, Shakespeare holds Leontes up to scornful laughter with Antigonus's concluding comment:

Leontes   Come, follow us;
    We are to speak in public; for this business
    Will raise us all.
Antigonus   To laughter, as I take it,
    If the good truth were known.

Scene Two

I

That Leontes is his own Iago is a thought that may well have occurred to Shakespeare when he made Antigonus rail against the villainous abuser of his king:

> It is for you we speak, not for ourselves:
> You are abus'd, and by some putter-on
> That will be damn'd for't: would I knew the villain,
> I would lam-damn him.   (II, i, 140)

The situation is highly reminiscent of Emilia's much more vehement denunciation, in her husband's presence, of the unknown villain who has abused Othello (*Oth.* IV, ii, 130ff.), ending with these words:

> The Moor's abus'd by some most villainous knave,
> Some base notorious knave, some scurvy fellow.
> O heavens, that such companions thou'dst unfold,
> And put in every honest hand a whip
> To lash the rascals naked through the world
> Even from the east to th' west.

This recollection, crossing his mind in the previous scene, may have suggested the name Emilia to Shakespeare when he decided to oblige Paulina to communicate with Hermione through a trusty and dear—and not merely anonymous—gentlewoman. But this is a trifle. The business of this scene is to introduce Paulina.

39

II

The gaoler in *Pandosto* overhears Bellaria's 'bitter complaints' when she finds herself quick with child. He goes and tells the king, hoping that he will in consequence 'somewhat appease his fury and release her' (p. 192). The office, as Paulina says, 'Becomes a woman best', and this is her immediate *raison d'être*. It is of course the baby itself and not the news that a baby is on the way that Paulina will bring the king. That news is already out, and has served the dramatist well. The action is now advanced to the more crucial time of the baby's birth. The king has rejected it in advance:

> let her sport herself
> With that she's big with; for 'tis Polixenes
> Has made thee swell thus. (II, i, 60)

It needs, therefore, an exceptionally masterful woman to confront Leontes with the child, and to raise in the audience any expectation that she will be successful in her mission. That is precisely what Paulina is: a masterful woman.

The germ of the character may be found in Mopsa (wife of the shepherd Porrus in *Pandosto*), before she is sweetened by the sight of gold. When her husband finds the infant Fawnia and brings her home, Mopsa is presented in a mood and situation suggestive in terms of bucolic comedy of those we find in the next scene of the play, between Paulina and Leontes:

> but as women are naturally given to believe the worst, so his wife, thinking it was some bastard, began to crow against her goodman, and taking up a cudgel (for the most master went breechless), swore solemnly that she would make clubs trumps if he brought any bastard brat within her doors. The goodman, seeing his wife in her majesty with her mace in her hand, thought it was time to bow for fear of her blows, and desired her to be quiet, for there was none such matter. (p. 200)

As the pastime of an idle moment the thought of such a woman was good fun, then as now. She could even make an acceptable basis for an entire play, if she were tamed at the end and preached orthodox doctrine to the unregererate (*T. Shrew* V, ii, 155). But taken seriously she was a menace:

> A woman impudent and mannish grown
> Is not more loath'd than an effeminate man
> In time of action. (*T.C.* III, iii, 217)

That is the point: man has his sphere and aptitudes, woman has hers; and normally they should not greatly overlap. But there were exceptional women, from Queen Elizabeth down, and for them allowance had to be made.[1] Such an exceptional case is Paulina, capable, obviously the dominant partner, and of conspicuous goodness. She is the Prospero of the play, carrying a great deal of the action on her shoulders and directing its course. As in *Lear* so in *The Winter's Tale* much of the characterization has an abstract quality. Hermione is honour, and hopeful patience; Leontes tyranny, then humility; Paulina militant goodness throughout.

She is, however, no woman impudent and mannish grown, but one who in the service of the right exercises a man's determination of character. When she enters the play she is at once mistress of the situation, boldly undertaking with a woman's tenderness to confront the lunatic king (30) with his new-born baby:

> We do not know [she says]
> How he may soften at the sight o' th' child:
> The silence often of pure innocence
> Persuades when speaking fails. (39)

Emilia strongly approves:

> there is no lady living
> So meet for this great errand, (43)

so evident is her honour and her goodness. It is left to Paulina herself, of course, to indicate her intended method of approach, which indeed is speaking, not silence:

> If I prove honey-mouth'd, let my tongue blister,
> And never to my red-look'd anger be
> The trumpet any more. (33)
> I'll use that tongue I have: if wit flow from't
> As boldness from my bosom, let't not be doubted
> I shall do good. (52)

---

[1] Cf. James E. Phillips, *Huntington Library Quarterly*, V (1941–2), 5–32, 211–34, on the subject of women rulers.

In this she is in evident contrast with conventional ideals of womanly excellence (cf. 'Her voice was ever soft, Gentle and low'), and, so considered, the part contains an inherent element of comedy.

Scene Three

I

Paulina's decision will express itself in prompt action. She will come at once to accomplish her mission, dominating the scene for half its length, as the positive champion of new life. Now therefore, before she comes, is the time to show Leontes' contrary condition —alone with his melancholy, heartless, vindictive, self-centred. The heavily stressed opening of his soliloquy, and the short, choppy phrases that follow, well express his restless, distraught state. He is negative, the victim of his own tyrannical weakness, thinking that he can prove himself strong by destroying life. Polixenes is too mighty to attack, but Hermione is within his power: therefore she must be burnt (1, 20, 26, 8). His intended revenge is untouched by noble sentiment. He serves no imagined cause, has no pity for anyone but himself. No one can outwit or make a mock of *him* with impunity (24): his motives are those of a schoolboy coward.

Yet Shakespeare cannot damn his hero absolutely by completely drying up human sentiment in him. Some seed of salvation must survive. This is his love of Mamillius, whose sickness the dramatist invents and significantly involves at this point in the complex of Leontes' thoughts, motives and actions. The servant delivers his message in the middle of the king's broodings. But it comes as no surprise to him; it is no chance interruption. Leontes is deeply concerned about the boy and is keeping himself informed of every change in his condition (10, 18). But his loving care only sharpens his sense of dishonour and need of revenge, for in his state of vindictive obsession he blames Hermione for Mamillius's illness: conceiving the dishonour of his mother, Leontes says, the boy

> took it deeply,
> Fasten'd and fix'd the shame on't in himself.   (12)

The passage is a vital one for the play as a whole. It postulates an ideal harmony and integrity in the family relationship in accordance with which an injury to one member affects all the others. Hermione is dishonoured: Mamillius falls ill. In the central scene of the play Hermione is further threatened: Mamillius dies: Hermione dies. So with Perdita, to whose fortunes we shall now be turning. She is cast out: and consequently the continued existence of the family itself is in jeopardy.

II

Now enters Paulina, that redoubtable lady, so plainly right-minded that she must be given her head. 'What!' says Leontes to Antigonus:

<pre>
                        canst not rule her?
Paulina   From all dishonesty he can: in this—
             Unless he take the course that you have done,
             Commit me for committing honour—trust it,
             He shall not rule me.
Antigonus   La you now, you hear:
             When she will take the rein I let her run;
             But she'll not stumble.   (46)
</pre>

She forces her way into the royal presence, Antigonus and other lords, in obedience to the king's command, trying to keep her out, but in vain. Only a virtuous lady fearless in the performance of good works could overawe Leontes in such a way that he cowers in impotent rage before her, spluttering ineffectual threats. Only a Paulina could bang the baby on his doorstep as it were, like a suffragette daring the whole police force to make her move along. From that on she takes charge of the play.

In her goodness she is, like Cordelia, a physician (*K.L.* I, i, 158):

<pre>
                        I
             Do come with words as medicinal as true,
             Honest as either, to purge him of that humour
             That presses him from sleep.   (36)
</pre>

Like Kent she is unmannerly only when the king is mad (71), and to the king's true self professes herself a 'loyal servant' and 'obedient counsellor' (53), speaking out for his own good. Her similarity in function and standpoint to Camillo is evident, and it is noteworthy that when he goes out of the play she comes into it. Having no place at court her attitude to the king can be blunter and more direct than his and she will not be cowed. When Camillo spoke of 'the good queen' (I, ii, 220) he was silenced by Leontes' contradiction. Not so Paulina:

> *Paulina*   I say, I come
> From your good queen.
> *Leontes*   Good queen!
> *Paulina*   Good queen, my lord, good queen, I say good queen,
> And would by combat make her good, so were I
> A man, the worst about you.[1]   (58)

It may also be said that she assumes, much more forcibly, the role of Antigonus in the scene before last, now that like the other lords he appears in more submissive mood. Once she almost echoes his very words, bringing to notice once more the multiplicity of the king's sin: Leontes is the only traitor in the court, she says:

>   for he
> The sacred honour of himself, his queen's,
> His hopeful son's, his babe's, betrays to slander,
> Whose sting is sharper than a sword's.
>   (83; cf. II, i, 127)

Later, when she calls Leontes 'a most unworthy and unnatural lord' (113), he threatens to have her burnt, for treason. 'I care not', she replies,

> It is an heretic that makes the fire,
> Not she which burns in't.

Instantly, that is to say, she interprets his threat in the spirit of militant martyrdom. Her first allegiance is to truth, and if she is to burn, it must be because of that allegiance. An outspoken character delivering home truths with impunity is usually of greatest service to a dramatist as a means of giving information to the audience; and this in due course Paulina will indeed be called upon to do. For the present, however, her function (besides that of delivering the baby) has been to impress us with her honesty,

---

[1] This thought looks very much like the transposition into serious, courtly terms of Greene's Mopsa 'in her majesty with her mace in her hand', prepared to make clubs trumps.

goodness, and fearless strength of character so that we may believe her implicitly when she does give us fresh information.

In the bustle of Paulina's exit (made in the spirit of 'Hands off: don't push me: I'm going')—corresponding after a fashion to the headlong haste of Polixenes' and Camillo's departure—we will in the theatre overlook the reflection that she is leaving the baby to its fate and should perhaps rather have considered taking it away with her. But she does not leave it without the prayer that Jove may send it 'A better guiding spirit' than its father.

As for Leontes, she departs leaving his dangerous, unsafe lunes to the 'tender' care of the lords, who she is sure

> Will never do him good, not one of you.   (127)

She will herself shortly be taking over the king's guidance, but as it turns out her scorn of the lords is not altogether well placed. For they do presently dissuade Leontes from his horrible purpose (150); and, unlikely as he may seem thus far in the scene to play the part of Jove's 'guiding spirit', it is Antigonus who stakes his life (161, 166) 'To save the innocent'. The point is emphasized by giving him, when he accepts his fearful errand, a prayer in harmony with Paulina's:

> Come on, poor babe;
> Some powerful spirit instruct the kites and ravens
> To be thy nurses.   (184)

III

When we first met him Antigonus won our respect. In this scene as a henpecked husband he must to some extent be a figure of fun. But it is Leontes who treats him as such—

> Thou dotard! Thou art woman-tir'd, unroosted
> By thy dame Partlet here—   (74)

and the spirit in which he does so is much the same as the spirit in which he plucks his beard (161). So, like his grim little jest at the end of Scene i, Antigonus's situation here is not one of unmixed comedy. Yet undeniably in the earlier part of the scene he does look amusingly weak beside Paulina's strength (30, 44, 50, 109); and this good, rather comical old man is the only serious character in the play for whom an 'Exit pursued by a bear' would be conceivable.

His wife's mastery of manner is her salvation (and the play's): she escapes unscathed from Leontes' anger. But the lords remain behind. They are courtiers, and however much they may speak out they are the king's men. When Antigonus is ordered to have the child burnt the lords, kneeling, dissuade Leontes from his purpose, but charged to swear on the king's sword to do his bidding his liege man cannot choose but do so. Antigonus is a willing sacrifice:

> I'll pawn the little blood which I have left
> To save the innocent. (165)

And so he takes up the child—whom the king still dubs a 'female bastard' (174; cf. 75, 160)—thus placing himself under his wife's curse:

>   For ever
> Unvenerable be thy hands, if thou
> Tak'st up the princess, by that forced baseness
> Which he has put upon't. (77)

With ironic faith in the kindness of wolves and bears he goes forth, the good old man invoking blessings not only on the child's head but on the king's (186).

IV

Without waiting for the oracle, and profanely assuming the child's bastardy, Leontes has sent Antigonus off to

> commend it strangely to some place
> Where chance may nurse or end it.

No sooner has he done so than word comes that posts 'are come / An hour since' to say that Cleomenes and Dion have landed with the oracle and are hasting to the court. Does Shakespeare wish us to understand that, by delaying the news by an hour, chance was giving Leontes time to seal his own fate and that of the child, which hung so precariously in the balance: 'better burn it now . . . let it live. / It shall not neither'? It may be so, but we could wish that the evidence were clearer.

46

The scene ends as it began, with Leontes' hunger for his wife's death, to assuage the tumult of his mind. Even before his emissaries return to court with the oracle he arranges for the trial of 'Our most disloyal lady'. She shall, he says, have

> A just and open trial. While she lives
> My heart will be a burden to me.   (204)

Thus once more, deluding himself that he is fair and just, he arrogantly puts his own blind forejudgement before the pronouncement of Apollo.

Act Three   Scene One

This, like the opening scenes of the previous acts, imparts a sense of normality, of happiness, contrasting with what has been or is to come. Like them it is brief and intimate. The glimpse of Cleomenes and Dion on their way home from the port brings a serene and gentle air, very welcome after the vehemence of Paulina, the rage of Leontes, the spectacle of an infant about to be burnt or exposed. The delicate climate of the isle, the 'celestial habits' and reverence of the priests, the unearthliness of the sacrifice, the thunderous voice of the Oracle: these induce a mood of confidence and a sense of mystery and spiritual support. Cleomenes and Dion are disturbed by the news of proclamations against the queen, but as their journey has been fortunate so the issue of it, they hope, will be 'gracious' for her. With that sentiment, and with a hint—ironic in the event—that we may expect 'something rare' to 'rush to knowledge' when the oracle is read, we end the scene refreshed and hopeful.[1]

Scene Two

I

To this central scene the culminating action of the first movement of the play is assigned: Hermione is put on trial and dies. The

[1] In Greene (p. 196) the deputation to the Oracle quickly makes the journey, 'desirous to see the situation and custom of the island'. It returns 'with great triumph'. Shakespeare with the dramatist's instinct for immediacy shows it only once—hastening back well pleased, within a short distance of the court, and discussing what it has seen.

In Greene the deputation numbers six, 'scarce indifferent men in the queen's behalf'. In Shakespeare the number is two. Besides answering theatrical convenience the smaller number makes for dramatic economy, for intimacy, brevity, and concentration of effect, especially as the two men are, like the audience, strong for the queen.

scene falls into three sections. The first consists chiefly of Hermione's speech in her own defence and ends with the reading of the oracle and the momentary rejoicing (137). The second covers the death of Mamillius, the apparent death of Hermione, Leontes' intended reconciliation and his public confession (172). In the third Hermione's death is confirmed, and Leontes resolves upon a life of unbroken remorse.

II

The first section depends for its inspiration on the two trial scenes in *Pandosto*, which are very different in character and spirit. The earlier of these is dramatic, dividing the interest between the two contestants—the king vindictive, on the attack, the queen spirited, holding her own. In the second trial (the trial by oracle, as we might call it), the emphasis is almost entirely on the queen, who alone speaks after the reading of the indictment, until she refers herself to the oracle. Shakespeare contrives to combine the effect of these contrasting scenes while transforming them.

Leontes opens the proceedings with a short speech. Still anxious to clear himself of tyranny he makes a virtue of the open trial, of which Hermione will soon express a very different view (41, 105). Otherwise this speech and the order summoning the session (II, iii, 201), which may still be ringing in our ears, have nothing in common. 'Our most disloyal lady' Leontes now talks of as 'one / Of us too much belov'd'. Instead of

> While she lives
> My heart will be a burden to me

he says

> This sessions (to our great grief we pronounce)
> Even pushes 'gainst our heart.

This is plain hypocrisy. Shakespeare is using false profession of love and regret to damn the man still further in our eyes; and throughout this section he continues to present him in the same unsympathetic light.[1]

---

[1] At the outset of his jealousy we get a glimpse of how greatly Leontes had loved his wife when Polixenes tells Camillo of his meeting with him:

This part of the scene is dominated by Hermione. Her answer to the charges against her is what matters. This speech may be seen as an extended version (given variety, warmer feeling, poetry) of Bellaria's 'cheerful reply' (p. 197) at her second trial, punctuated by spiteful interruptions from Leontes (54, 84) mainly based on a 'rough reply' of Pandosto's at the first trial (p. 195). It embraces the whole of Bellaria's set speech, closely re-writing her impressive opening words, ending with her appeal to the divine oracle, and following the routine lines of her central section in defence of her probity of thought and purpose. All this accounts for about half of Hermione's speech. It is the other half—what Shakespeare adds—that is of greatest interest.

It must be seen in the light of its introduction, based on *Pandosto*:[1]

> . . . if powers divine
> Behold our human actions (as they do),
> I doubt not then but innocence shall make
> False accusation blush, and tyranny
> Tremble at patience.   (28)

This is a public affirmation of confidence grounded in religious faith, easy for one to make for whom it is a rule of life. So far the speech is in accord with Bellaria's 'cheerful reply', and the note of fundamental certitude returns in the concluding appeal:

> I do refer me to the oracle:
> Apollo be my judge!   (115)

But what lies between is by no means 'cheerful'. Hermione, unlike Bellaria at this point, is a human being. Honourable grief has burnt

---

[1] The opening section of Bellaria's speech reads as follows:
If the divine powers be privy to human actions—as no doubt they are—I hope my patience shall make fortune blush, and my unspotted life shall stain spiteful discredit. For although lying report hath sought to appeach mine honour, and suspicion hath intended to soil my credit with infamy, yet where virtue keepeth the fort, report and suspicion may assail, but never sack. (p. 197)

> The king hath on him such a countenance
> As he had lost some province, and a region
> Lov'd as he loves himself;   (I, ii, 368)

but once he is jealous there is no vestige of love in him at all. His self-induced jealousy is a different condition from Othello's: the retribution he intends is not undertaken like Othello's as a sacred duty and hence is not mingled with pity and regret as his is: it is merely selfish and vindictive.

yet further into her breast. She has now had her child, and it has, she believes, been sent to its death. Innocence and patience will undoubtedly triumph, but this thought is no remedy for her present unhappiness,

> which is more
> Than history can pattern, though devis'd
> And play'd to take spectators. (35)

Her strong statement of general belief gives no indication of her actual condition of bewilderment and emptiness of spirit. Its buoyant certitude of rhythm takes no account of the battering her sensitive nature has received, or the stunned, helpless state of her mind, unable to take in what is happening:

> Sir,
> You speak a language that I understand not. (80)
> To me life can be no commodity;
> The crown and comfort of my life, your favour,
> I do give lost, for I do feel it gone,
> But know not how it went. (93)

What joy or comfort has she left to live for?—she goes on—deprived, she knows not how, of her husband's favour ('The crown and comfort of my life'), barred 'like one infectious' from the first-fruits of her body, and her baby from her breast

> (The innocent milk in it most innocent mouth)
> Hal'd out to murder.

Those she has lost she feels as extensions of her own person. Most of the indignities she has suffered are physical indignities (102). She has been deeply, irreparably wounded and pained. Even as she awaits the judgement of Apollo she can think only of the indignity of her trial, so unbefitting her birth and station, and the pitiful flatness of her misery (119). It was his mother's dishonour, Leontes asserted, that Mamillius felt so deeply in himself that he fell ill. Now Hermione powerfully reinforces that conception of family unity, giving it her own characteristic emphasis. As a mother she is deeply conscious of the physical nature of the family bond. As a great lady she is keenly conscious of the dignity and honour of place and lineage and the obligations that they entail. For her,

> A fellow of the royal bed, which owe
> A moiety of the throne, a great king's daughter,
> The mother of a hopeful prince,

the greatest dishonour would be that her 'near'st of kin' should 'Cry fie upon [her] grave' (53).

III

The second phase of the scene consists of a rapid succession of surprising incidents—Leontes' rejection of the oracle, the report of Mamillius's death, Hermione's seizure, Leontes' confession. This alters the order of events given in *Pandosto*.[1] There after the reading of the oracle the king confesses, then the boy dies, and then the queen: the boy's death, designed to cause the queen's death from shock, is not itself sufficiently motivated. (If it is intended as a punishment upon the king for his past crimes—as may afterwards obscurely appear—it shows up Apollo as 'slack to plague such offences' (p. 198) in waiting until after his victim has seen the error of his ways.) Shakespeare makes the matter perfectly clear. Instead of accepting the oracle and confessing, Leontes rejects it and orders the sessions to proceed. Instantly news is brought of Mamillius's death, and though he knows that the boy has been sick he interprets his death as a sign of Apollo's anger (146). Thus an immediately clear and dramatically effective reason for Mamillius's death is provided, and a strong link also between Leontes' impiety and the death of Hermione.[2]

---

[1] In *Pandosto* after the oracle was read there was great rejoicing that the queen's name was cleared:

But the king . . . was so ashamed . . . that he entreated his nobles to persuade Bellaria to forgive and forget these injuries; promising . . . to reconcile himself to Egistus and Franion. . . . As thus he was relating [his plot against Egistus], there was word brought that his young son Garinter was suddenly dead, which news so soon as Bellaria heard, surcharged before with extreme joy and now suppressed with heavy sorrow, her vital spirits were so stopped that she fell down presently dead, and could be never revived. (pp. 197–8)

[2] It is not impossible that it was the momentary expectation of a contrary rather than a contrasting statement after Greene's words 'But the king' (see above, in footnote 1) that first suggested to Shakespeare that here was a neat

In replacing the king's confession by his profane order to continue the sessions Shakespeare reserves the confession for the end of this section. For the queen's death must follow immediately upon her son's as in Greene (just as Mamillius's must immediately follow the flouting of the oracle), so that its consequential character may be given full dramatic force. At the same time it must not be allowed to rob Mamillius's death of all independent dramatic impact. Hence Shakespeare divides the death of Hermione into two stages. In the first she is removed to have restoratives applied; in the second her death is confirmed. These two stages are separated by Leontes' confession, so as to mark off for independent elaboration the confirmation of Hermione's death and its consequences. They are the important things. Shakespeare is careful, therefore, not to treat the public confession as much more than a necessary passage of transition, to lull us into a state of sufficient unpreparedness for Paulina's theatrical return. For this purpose he diverts our mind from Hermione and on to Camillo. Even her children are unmentioned, and she receives just half a line (156), sandwiched between 'I'll reconcile me to Polixenes' and 'recall the good Camillo', whereas Camillo gets three-quarters of the speech. As he is shortly to return to active prominence in the play it is perhaps a useful enough thing to be reminded of his virtues. To end this section of the scene these are contrasted with Leontes' sin, which is now to become the special object of attention:

> how he glisters
> Thorough my rust! and how his piety
> Does my deeds make the blacker![1]

[1] As for the phrase 'New woo my queen', it reveals in passing that Leontes does not share Pandosto's crass and offensive expectation that his noble, sensitive wife, so deeply injured, *could* come leaping back into his arms when he whistled to her—and whistled by proxy. But as Hermione is about to be reported dead, the dramatist touches on the possibility of reconciliation only thus briefly and incidentally.

place to start altering the order of events: there was general rejoicing, *but the king*, not believing the oracle, ordered the sessions to proceed.

Shakespeare's habit of laying his mind open to suggestions from the book in front of him is further illustrated in this connexion, for, as we have seen, Leontes' great profaneness 'gainst the oracle is adumbrated in *Pandosto* when the king on being told that the queen was with child swore that both of them 'should die if the gods themselves said no'.

The idea of dealing with the queen's death in two stages may have arisen out of the parallel passage in *Pandosto*, where Bellaria 'fell down presently dead, and could be never revived'. That may be said to correspond exactly to Shakespeare's treatment of the case: Paulina claims that

> This news is mortal to the queen: look down
> And see what death is doing;

but Leontes thinks she will recover and asks that 'Some remedies for life' be applied.

It is a curious expression, however, and may have played a further part in Shakespeare's creative process: 'fell down presently dead, and could be never revived'. Bellaria, when the guard came to the prison to take away her baby, 'fell down in a swound, so that all thought she had been dead'; but at last she came to herself, delivered a speech, again fell down in a trance, was revived, lost her memory, and 'lay for a great time without moving, as one in a trance'. After that, her final failure to be revived seems almost out of character, open to doubt. Suppose Hermione fell down presently dead and *could* eventually be revived. After all, Pericles thought Thaisa dead. And what about Jupiter's message to Posthumus—'branches, which, being dead many years, shall after revive'?

IV

Pandosto's true repentance comes after the queen's death. He spends three days in speechless swoon. Then, deeply troubled by the effects of his suspicion, jealousy, unnatural actions and cause-less cruelty, and his mind set on suffering due retribution, he 'as in a fury brayed out' bitter speeches against himself, as forced in style as the account of his public pronouncement was matter-of-fact:

> O miserable Pandosto! what surer witness than conscience? I have committed such a bloody fact, as repent I may, but recall I cannot. . . . Are the gods just? then let them revenge such brutish cruelty. My innocent babe I have drowned in the seas; my loving wife I have slain with slanderous suspicion; my trusty friend I have sought to betray, and yet the gods are slack to plague such offences. Ah, unjust

Apollo! Pandosto is the man that hath committed the fault; why should Garinter, silly child, abide the pain? Well, sith the gods mean to prolong my days to increase my dolour, I will offer my guilty blood a sacrifice to those sackless souls whose lives are lost by my rigorous folly. (p. 198)

It is with the substance and manner of this soliloquy, notably reorganized and transformed, that Shakespeare starts the last movement of the scene. He will not, like Greene, give the king two speeches of self-recrimination one on top of the other. Yet there are possibilities in this vigorous, hard-hitting stuff not lightly to be passed over. Whom should he give it to? Who would speak out thus against his sovereign? Who but the redoubtable Paulina? So Shakespeare lets the king's conscience, as revealed in Pandosto's soliloquy, speak out vengefully against him, through her. She now returns to report the death of Hermione, but not simply as the lady who has been absent from the stage since the queen's seizure, seeking to revive her. She is also retributive justice, knowing—along with all the other charges against him, which (like Pandosto) she lists—the detail that Paulina could not know, that Leontes would

> have poison'd good Camillo's honour
> To have him kill a king. (188)

Her dual functions are cunningly combined in the rhetoric of her speech (175–202). The heightened style of Pandosto's soliloquy is based on apostrophe and rhetorical question; Paulina's on *occupatio* and climax—the use of negation for positive effect is a characteristic device of hers (cf. 223–30, II, iii, 115). She is a Senecan *nuntius* spinning out the recital of the dreadful news not with gory details but with an indictment of the king arranged in a climax of negative propositions culminating in the announcement of the queen's death, the crime in comparison with which all Leontes' other offences seem of no account.

Thus the trial of Hermione resolves itself into the trial of Leontes. The true culprit is now being arraigned. The fundamental charge is tyranny, the charge of being the mad tyrannical fool of his own fancies (179ff.). This is the charge that Leontes was concerned to clear himself of (4; II, iii, 121), that Hermione made (31), and of which the oracle has already declared him guilty. But that was before the queen's death, the most monstrous consequence of his tyrannical abuses (190). To some of these he has already confessed, and they are all set out in order of mounting monstrosity in the indictment—the betrayal of Polixenes, the attempt to poison Camillo's honour, the exposure of his baby daughter,

> Nor is't directly laid to thee the death
> Of the young prince: . . .
> . . . . . . this is not, no,
> Laid to thy answer; but the last—O lords,
> When I have said, cry 'woe!'—the queen, the queen,
> The sweet'st, dear'st creature's dead: and vengeance for't
> Not dropp'd down yet.

Thus consistently addressing the king as thou—as the queen was addressed as thou in *her* indictment (13)—Justice prefers the charges, waiving them all except the last, which seems to cry to heaven for instant vengeance.

Yet though she is Justice here and Honour and Goodness all the time Paulina is still a human being: a woman concerned about an ill-treated baby, about the gross injustice of its mother's defamation, about the father's insane jealousy and stupidity. An audacious lady of boundless tongue, she uses 'the boldness of her speech' (218) in the hope of doing good (II, ii, 52; II, iii, 42, 91). Here, where—to subserve and emphasize her function as a dramatic device—she even thous her sovereign, she may be explained as taking a calculated risk so as (if she succeeds) the more completely to establish moral ascendancy over him. This she does; and when she does so she resumes her (elsewhere invariable) deferential modes of address (226).

Let us return now to the implication the scene contains that Leontes is on trial. If this is so, it may be said, one can understand why there is no defence, since there is an implicit plea of guilty; but why is there no sentence? Why has vengeance still not dropped down yet at the end of the scene? Because 'the rarer action is / In virtue than in vengeance'? Yes, that is possible. It was Leontes, blinded with jealousy, who looked for 'present vengeance' on his wife (II, iii, 22), and she who wished her father could see the flatness of her misery, 'yet with eyes / Of pity, not revenge' (123). It is to the tyrant with boiling oil (175) that Paulina comes to report the queen's death, but that is the Leontes of Hermione's trial (90), who has now confessed his black deeds (173)—due, he now sees, to his being 'transported by [his] jealousies / To bloody thoughts and to revenge' (158). Pandosto, condemning himself, eager to receive the gods' vengeance and impatient at their slackness, thinks to kill himself as a sacrifice to his victims. But Leontes has now come to himself: the scales have fallen from his eyes and he is a man of keen moral discernment (153ff.). So, arraigned before the bar of conscience, and humbled by the heavens' strokes in the death of Mamillius, he is most unlikely to take the judgement of his case out of the gods' hands. Revenge, no, not by his own hand; but pity? Is he deserving of that?

Paulina is taking no chances. She tests him at every stage. Her words are at once an incentive and a deterrent. If Leontes still has the mind of a tyrant he may, excited by her rant (175), her display of emotion, out-Herod Herod, as she incites him to do (183). If he is truly purged of his tyranny his reaction may be the opposite, and he may readily put himself under her guidance, but if he is obdurate he will think his crimes too terrible to be atoned for, and will lose himself in despair. So again she tests him, seeming to urge him to harden his heart:

> But, O thou tyrant!
> Do not repent these things, for they are heavier
> Than all thy woes can stir: therefore betake thee
> To nothing but despair. A thousand knees
> Ten thousand years together, naked, fasting,
> Upon a barren mountain, and still winter
> In storm perpetual, could not move the gods
> To look that way thou wert.[1]   (207)

But he responds as a penitent humbly submitting himself to the scourge, even to the scourge of Paulina's words—formerly his abomination, which, to test him, she has represented as themselves deserving torture (177)—

[1] This is a tendentious statement of the doctrine lightly enunciated by Prospero at the end of *The Tempest*:

> And my ending is despair,
> Unless I be reliev'd by prayer,
> Which pierces so that it assaults
> Mercy itself and frees all faults.

In the relaxed mood of that epilogue plenary indulgence may even be hoped for:

> As you from crimes would pardon'd be,
> Let your indulgence set me free.

> Go on, go on:
> Thou canst not speak too much; I have deserv'd
> All tongues to talk their bitt'rest.   (214)

So far, so good. The tables are turned. He appears to be penitent. But how settled is his penitence? May it not be like Pandosto's
hasty superficiality when he imagined that, the queen's name
having been cleared, his nobles could at once persuade her to
forgive and forget her injuries? So Paulina changes her tune.[1]
Leontes is no longer a tyrant but her royal liege (226), 'touch'd /
To th' noble heart' (221); she is no longer inflexible Justice ('A
thousand knees . . .') but a rash and foolish woman, sorry for
having spoken as she did, for having touched his heart. Of course
that was wrong:

> What's gone and what's past help
> Should be past grief. Do not receive affliction
> At my petition.   (222)

Leontes should forget his wife, and punish or forgive Paulina for
reminding him of her. Thus, starting with the thought of how
impossible it is for him to move the gods, she encourages him by
negation and apparent dissuasion to nourish his griefs, to receive
affliction, and to welcome reminders of what he might forget. The
final weapon in Paulina's armoury is her deliberate display of
human weakness, showing by example how hard even she finds it
to live up to her own ostensible preaching, and how natural it is
for one's thoughts to turn unbidden to lost love and spouse and
children:

[1] J. H. P. Pafford (p. lii) raises the question 'Why did Paulina have such a
sudden change in her attitude to Leontes?' and equates it with 'Why did
Leontes become jealous?' In answer he says it is easy to make too much of
motivation: if such events are accepted by an audience nothing is wrong.
Camillo did not know how or why Leontes' suspicions had grown: action
mattered more to him at the time than explanations. 'So with the audience—
their minds are engaged with what is happening, what is coming, not with
searching for reasons'. The two questions, I submit, are different in kind. For
a *pattern* of conduct, motives may be too complex or too deeply buried in the
recesses of character to disengage or define. Hamlet does not know his motive,
Shylock can give no reason, Iago can give too many; and this the dramatist
tells us. But in the case of a simple matter like a character's sudden change of
attitude, we should certainly expect a relatively simple explanation to emerge.
If we fail to find it, it may indeed not be there, but it is dangerous to content
ourselves with that assumption.

> Now, good my liege,
> Sir, royal sir, forgive a foolish woman:
> The love I bore your queen—lo, fool again!
> I'll speak of her no more, nor of your children:
> I'll not remember you of my own lord
> (Who is lost too).

This, then, is Leontes' self-determined sentence—a life-time of penitence, Paulina keeping keen his grief and shame. Hermione and Mamillius are to be buried together.

> Once a day I'll visit
> The chapel where they lie, and tears shed there
> Shall be my recreation. So long as nature
> Will bear up with this exercise, so long
> I daily vow to use it. Come, and lead me
> To these sorrows.[1]

Through that exercise Leontes will in due time move the gods to look his way and will bring tincture and lustre to Hermione's lip and eye.[2]

V

As the keystone of a tragi-comedy this central scene is admirably contrived. Hitherto full tragic emphasis has been avoided. In II, i, the impact of Leontes' hubris was softened by giving him some

---

[1] Greene provides the suggestion for this:
This epitaph being engraven, Pandosto would once a day repair to the tomb, and there with watery plaints bewail his misfortune, coveting no other companion but sorrow, nor no other harmony but repentance. (p. 199)

[2] At l. 199 Paulina turned to the lords to announce the queen's death, and one of them expostulated in horror at the news. 'I'll say she's dead', she assured him:

> I'll swear't. If word nor oath
> Prevail not, go and see: if you can bring
> Tincture or lustre in her lips, her eye,
> Heat outwardly or breath within, I'll serve you
> As I would do the gods.   (203)

These lines were addressed to the lord (*you*, 204) or perhaps to the company at large, not specifically to the king, whom she continues to tax as 'thou tyrant' in ll. 207ff.; but the words are of course quite general in their application.

show of deference to the god in consulting the oracle (189); and the mitigating comment of scornful laughter was at hand (198)— as was the distraction of a domestic comedy note (Chaunticlere unroosted by dame Partlet) in II, iii. At every stage the sense of Leontes' inhumanity has been vocal, sharing attention, exposing him as terrible but contemptible, and *un*representative of the human condition. Now attention is concentrated, for here is unmistakable crisis. The business must be cleared or ended (III, i, 18). The queen's plight and the king's disease have come to a head: she is on trial for her life, he bent on taking it. The constituents of high tragedy are present, in undisputed possession. Besides the tyrannical victim of senseless jealous frenzy and its innocent cause, there are also involved, off stage, that small annexment Mamillius, and the great god Apollo, indeed 'the heavens themselves' (137, 146), ready to strike. This they are not slow to do when Leontes' self-sufficiency breaks all bounds in unequivocal impiety—

> There is no truth at all i' th'oracle:
> The sessions shall proceed: this is mere falsehood.

The business is cleared, but is not to be ended thus. The death of Mamillius is not the central thing. It is not with that that Leontes is directly charged. It is the death of Hermione, and that comes later, after an interval in which we are lulled into a sense of false security. Hermione does not die on the stage.[1] As a substitute, Paulina is given a speech of melodramatic rhetoric, casting the news of Hermione's death in the form of a catalogue of charges against Leontes. The news must even for contemporary playgoers familiar with *Pandosto* have been a devastating blow, and any audience will willingly be stirred to participate in Paulina's fury. The heavens, we note, have not struck again; but undoubtedly Leontes must pay. In taking on this moralistic, legalistic colouring the tragic mood diminishes.

The accuser of the earlier part of the scene is now the accused. But the situation has undergone another change affecting the tone

---

[1] It is important that she should not do so, for that would oblige the audience to witness, and confirm as actual, an event whose truth it must afterwards be in a position to accept as not actual but figurative.

The stage persons silently concur in the king's belief that Hermione has only fainted—all but Paulina. Making her say at this point that the queen is dying helps to authenticate for the audience her later report of the death.

of the play still more profoundly. Before Paulina's return Leontes has already repudiated the tyrannies of which she comes to accuse him, though he cannot of course disclaim their consequences. Spiritually he is now her ally. He who scorned Antigonus for being 'woman-tir'd' now humbly bows to Paulina's rule. Here is no tragic irony: tragi-comic is the word. Retributive Justice, dropping the expectation of instant vengeance (201), prepares the way instead for a lifetime of sorrow and penance, freely undertaken. The spirit of Hermione, that 'Of pity, not revenge', is in the ascendant.

Scene Three

I

Greene passes from the matter of Pandosto to the matter of Fawnia in a sentence:

> But leaving him to his dolorous passions, at last let us come to show the tragical discourse of the young infant.

His 'discourse of the young infant' is 'tragical' only in its initial stages, when the baby is driven in an unguided boat across the seas at the mercy of a tempest; after that all goes most fortunately for her. For the dramatist's purpose the early part is all that is of value: the tempest, the coming to land, the shepherd's finding the child, his kindness, his cupidity, and the consequent secrecy. Using human agency in the person of Antigonus, Shakespeare can give the incident a more truly 'tragical' quality. These events happen hard upon the king's conversion and will go well in the same act with it, to balance Scene i. The rustic, superstitious gladness of its conclusion in the midst of death (as Shakespeare contrives it) stands in ironic contrast with the courtly and reverential optimism on the brink of disaster in that earlier scene.

II

Hermione is dead. Everything confirms it. Leontes sees her dead (III, ii, 234). She and Mamillius are buried in one grave. Her death

62

is attested by Paulina, the embodiment of truth. In her last lines Paulina speaks of her husband as 'lost too', and in this next scene her words come true, but not before Antigonus brings to mind the dream he has had the previous night, which convinces him also that 'Hermione hath suffer'd death' (41). In the dream Hermione appeared to him as a spirit from the dead, with the forced, theatrical air of a Senecan ghost:

> thrice bow'd before me,
> And, gasping to begin some speech, her eyes
> Became two spouts; the fury spent, anon
> Did this break from her.

Having made her speech, 'with shrieks / She melted into air'. Though her gasps and gushing tears recall Bellaria not Hermione this is a perfectly orthodox stage ghost with all the conventional signs; and it is no wonder that Antigonus decides that it is a true ghost, and concludes that Hermione is dead. Not only the manner but the matter of her speech may seem to confirm this conclusion for the audience; for she appears to foretell Antigonus's death (35), and very soon he is indeed dead.

It is of course not to add one more item of evidence confirming Hermione's death that Shakespeare makes it seem to Antigonus that she has returned from beyond the grave endowed with supernatural understanding and foresight. The very theatricality of the ghost stamps it as a routine device, important not in itself but as a means to an end. That end is to show Hermione to be actively involved in the direction of her daughter's fate. Perdita is not put to sea without guidance and washed to the shores of Polixenes' kingdom by mere chance, as happens in *Pandosto*. She is in the charge of Antigonus, who finding that his ship 'hath touch'd upon / The deserts of Bohemia', decides to go ashore and leave her there, believing that to be Apollo's wish (43). This is not the result of whim or chance, but of Hermione's guiding hand. Antigonus's commission is vague: to commend the baby 'strangely to some place / Where chance may nurse or end it' (II, iii, 181). The vision of Hermione makes it more specific:

> Places remote enough are in Bohemia:
> There weep, and leave it crying.   (32)

These instructions Antigonus is punctilious to carry out. As the scene opens he is questioning a mariner to make sure that where they have landed is indeed the deserts of Bohemia, and just before his hasty exit he even remembers the injunction to weep, though his heart is too full to carry it out. It is, then, in obedience to Hermione, and to Apollo whom he believes to be prompting her in this, that the old man faithfully performs his distasteful task in the face of the approaching storm.

III

The apparition had convinced Antigonus not merely that Hermione was dead but that she had 'suffer'd death'—that is, that the oracle had condemned her and that she had been executed. How else, he evidently had argued with himself (38), could she have met her death? That was the only peril she was exposed to when he left Sicilia. And besides, why should she ask for her baby to be left in Bohemia, unless Polixenes was its father (43)?

It seems a sad indignity to impose on this loyal old character—the most vehement and outspoken of Hermione's champions among the courtiers—thus to make him at the last moment lose faith in her honour. It is sad, certainly, for his belief in her was his most positive characteristic; and there is deep pathos in his ironical recollection of the vision as it approached him

> in pure white robes
> *Like* very sanctity. (22)

If it is an indignity, however, the way in which he faces it gives him added dignity. He is the single-minded servant of truth, following it even to his own destruction. The gods have, he believes, shown seeming honour to be unchaste, and have disproved his most deep-felt faith: nevertheless 'Their sacred wills be done', even though in doing them he may be accursed (7, 52). The child he thought his master's is indeed, alas, the bastard brat it had been dubbed, but Antigonus is none the less zealous and pitiful in his concern for its comfort (46). We may see that he has increased in stature, but as for himself, he is heart-broken. His sorrow is beyond tears, he says, 'But my heart bleeds'. He is, indeed, ripe for death. It would be cruel to keep him alive to learn how he had been deluded by logic; and the advanced age assigned to him makes him unlikely to survive so long. Hence suggestions from Greene—the 'wolves or eagles' which molest the sheep in his Sicilia, the 'mighty tempest' that drives the baby there in its unguided boat—combine to give the scene a menacing frame and background (3–13, 49, 54–6) of angry nature—not unconnected with the anger of the gods—out of which suddenly emerges the means of Antigonus's accidental death. There has been mounting tension as the old man methodically does what he has to do, noting the gathering storm and thinking only of the baby's welfare; pity has been aroused by the whole situation and by Antigonus's reactions to it; and admiration has been stimulated by his piety, loyalty and courage. But the total effect falls far short of tragic substance. He may think he is leaving the baby in jeopardy; and we know that his loss of faith in Hermione is mistaken. But these things are not central. What is central is that Antigonus offered to pawn the little blood he had left to save the innocent (II, iii, 166)—and that he now pays the forfeit. It was a deliberate offer of self-sacrifice, a clearly-understood bargain—one life, if required, for another—noble not tragic. An honest bargain faithfully carried out on both sides cannot be tragic. Antigonus gets what he wants. He saves the innocent. The sacrifice is well worth it. Besides, as we have noted, heart-broken and old he is ready for death when it comes.

Anything else would be out of place here. Antigonus is a minor character. The catastrophe of the incident is a minor catastophe. It marks the end of a movement not of the play. In keeping with that movement, in which both heroine and hero are last seen as the embodiment of sorrow (21; III, ii, 243), it is deeply pathetic.

IV

What, then, of the bear?

> A savage clamour!
> Well may I get aboard! This is the chase:
> I am gone for ever!
> *Exit pursued by a bear.*

Antigonus hears the bear roaring, sees he has no time to lose, hears the hunting horn and, as the bear appears, fleetingly sees the irony of his being the quarry's quarry. And then, the bear gaining on him as he leaves the stage, he realizes that he is doomed.

In that there can be nothing to laugh at, so long as we occupy ourselves with Antigonus alone. We have learnt to admire and respect this old man, and we can feel keenly the horror of his situation. On the other hand there is the excitement of horn, haloos, and rush of bear round and round the stage (whether bear or man dressed up it will be expected to give a run for its money); there is the amusement usually to be derived from a performing animal or a man performing as one;[1] there is the novelty of the incident, being so different from anything we have seen before in the play: all this will combine, with the shock of horror which we share with Antigonus, a shock of a different kind—that of delighted surprise.

So, as everyone knows, the key of the play is changed in a twinkling from sacrifice to ransom, from pathos not to fun pure and simple but to a sense of both at once. The transition is easily effected. We can laugh even while we feel for the old man, for we have laughed at and with him before while appreciating his worth. Moreover, before we hear the Clown's richly comic account of the deaths by sea and land old Antigonus is replaced on the stage by an old shepherd, who is moved to take up the child for pity (76), just as Antigonus was. The Antigonus spirit, that is

---

[1] The bear in *The Winter's Tale* has been associated with the bear in *Mucedorus*. That bear is the occasion of rough and tumble fun (the clown Mouse, going backwards, falls over her as she enters), of fear (she frightens the heroine), of delighted audience participation (the cowardly nobleman exits, as he entered, 'persued with a beare'), and of lofty courtesy as hero meets heroine: Mucedorus having slain the beast off stage—

> That cruell beast most mercelesse and fell,
> Which hath bereaued thousands of their liues—

offers its head to the lady, who is delighted to have it. Such a bear, especially in a play which was obviously 'destined by the publishers particularly for companies of humble pretensions' (*Shakespeare Apocrypha*, p. 424), is unlikely to have remained for long in performance as the she-bear of the printed texts. In Appendix II, I conjecture that Shakespeare's company took *Mucedorus* on tour in 1608. On tour they would certainly have used a human bear in that play—and also, no doubt, in its court performance, to enforce the element of ridicule. There is good reason, therefore, to suppose that the same kind of bear was used in *The Winter's Tale*. (The two ornamental white bears drawing Oberon's chariot in Jonson's masque are plainly irrelevant (cf. Chambers, IV, 35), except possibly as reminders of the more pertinent bear in *Mucedorus*.)

to say, lives on, in the Old Shepherd, in a world where there is no curse on one who does so, but rather rich reward.

V

After that lull, the Clown joins his father. 'What ail'st thou man?' asks the Old Shepherd, for the young man is plainly not feeling well. Sickened by the sight of the deaths by sea and land he is going to report? No: it is just that his head is going up and down with the tossing waves he has gazed at, and dizzied by the bewildering variety of events he has witnessed:

Clown I would you did but see how it [the sea] chafes, how it rages, how it takes up the shore! But that's not the point. O, the most piteous cry of the poor souls! Sometimes to see 'em, and not to see 'em: now the ship boring the moon with her main-mast, and anon swallowed with yest and froth, as you'd thrust a cork into a hogs-head. And then for the land-service, to see how the bear tore out his shoulder-bone, how he cried to me for help and said his name was Antigonus, a nobleman. But to make an end of the ship, to see how the sea flap-dragoned it: but first, how the poor souls roared, and the sea mocked them: and how the poor gentleman roared, and the bear mocked him, both roaring louder than the sea or weather.

Shepherd Name of mercy, when was this, boy?

Clown Now, now: I have not winked since I saw these sights: the men are not yet cold under water, nor the bear half dined on the gentleman: he's at it now.

Shepherd Would I had been by, to have helped the old man!

Clown I would you had been by the ship side, to have helped her: there your charity would have lacked footing.

Shepherd Heavy matters! heavy matters! (88)

Here is comedy of a high order. At first the Clown's mind sways responsive to the ubiquitous movement of the sea, interpenetrating both land and sky (84), which was the context of the sights he tells of. 'But that's not the point', he says, trying to collect himself and not to talk of the sea eating up the land; but the oscillation of nature keeps breaking in and taking possession of his mind and its processes. At one moment his thought is lofty: 'now the ship boring the moon with her main-mast'; at the next, low: 'and anon swallowed with yest and froth, as you'd thrust a cork into a hogshead'. From drink he passes to food—'And then for the land-service [of courses], to see how the bear tore out his shoulder bone'—and thence to a combination of both—'how the sea flap-dragoned it': gulped the ship down like a hot brandy raisin in a boisterous game; and that was the end of the ship. But not quite. The Clown's mental equipoise is now restored. His mind no longer oscillates between sea and land. It does not need to do so. For the two have joined forces. They are playing the same game. He can hear them at it. Appearing like a pageant snap-dragon brought to life, the sea reinforces the bestial aspect of nature, ready to tear men to pieces, and like the bear roars back at them in mockery of their impotence. Men and natural forces are at one only in contributing to riotous cacophony.

Thus the Clown's speech has a serious subject: the beast in nature, man's impotence in its hands, his pettiness in the context of natural forces. This is decently saved from unseasonable obtrusiveness, however, by throwing the emphasis on manner rather than matter, and by diverting attention to the speaker—a new character unlike any we have hitherto encountered in the play—and his reactions to the sights and sounds he tells of. Moreover the whole passage is a kind of dramatic parenthesis. The Old Shepherd has found the baby and is awaiting his opportunity to break the news to his son and to investigate.

Antigonus therefore has become variously subordinate in importance to other lines of interest. From one point of view he still shares attention with the baby ('things dying', 'things new born'), and he does so to the end of the scene; but his function and that of the mariners are now passive—to be disposed of, dismissed from the play, so that no one in Sicilia can know that the baby has been found; to do so *un*tragically (so as not to steal anyone's thunder), showing jointly that accidental death is not tragic, but only a monstrous mockery; and through the recital of their deaths to give prominence to new characters.

Finally, the parenthetical positioning of the Clown's speech has important structural consequences.

1. It enables us to meet the Old Shepherd first by himself. We see that in his different station of life he represents the same piety and humanity as Antigonus did in his. This eases the transition to

the new world as nothing else could; and as the good old man quickly finds the baby we can reassure ourselves on that score with the comfortable feeling that all will be well with her.

2. The delayed entrance of the Clown, heralded by exchange of shouts, gives him immediate and needed prominence, for he is the 'star turn' of the scene. In contrast with the Old Shepherd he is sophisticated and tough; later, in contrast with Autolycus, his situation will be reversed. Here he is not given, like his father, to rusticity of vocabulary and pious ejaculation, and he tempers his pity for those in misfortune (90, 98, 99) with common sense and even callousness (94, 104, 128), perhaps in the hope of irritating his unruffled father, whom he considers lazy and disposed to sentimental inertia (108, 134).[1]

3. The finding and the taking up of the baby need to be touched with a pretty light hand. The two events are all the better for being separated and hence diversified in treatment.

VI

The Antigonus theme is not laughed out of the play but rather is bowed out. The last line of the scene is

'Tis a lucky day, boy, and we'll do good deeds on't.

This as it were places the thoughts of 'things new born' and 'things dying' in causal relationship, very properly since without

---

[1] The psychology is sketched in with a deft comic hand. The son has been well brought up ('Now bless thyself: thou met'st with things dying'), but, as not infrequently happens in such a case, is watchful against parental encroachment on his individuality (126, 134). The father, superstitious ('it was told me I should be rich by the fairies'), and even rash and prodigal in his excitement ('Let my sheep go'), has nevertheless a true countryman's sense of property (which his son does not dispute), and well knows that the fairies help those who hold their tongues ('We are lucky, boy; and to be so still requires nothing but secrecy').

John Lawlor well notes in this connexion (p. 98):
> Greene's Shepherd wins his termagant wife's silence by telling her 'if she could hold her peace, they were made for ever'. But it is Shakespeare's 'Clown' who tells his father, 'You're a made old man'—to be answered, 'This is fairy gold, boy, and 'twill prove so'. The mercenary motive and the need for silence have been neatly fitted into place.

But the mercenary motive is not inconsistent with benevolence.

Antigonus's prepardness to die for Perdita she would not have
survived. The Old Shepherd and his son are 'lucky' (123) because,
having been prompted to take up the child for pity (76), they take
up with it 'fairy gold' (121): in gratitude they will do good deeds
on't. The first such 'good deed' (131) will be to give what remains
of Antigonus decent burial.

Act Four   Scene One

I

Like the 'prologue arm'd' in *Troilus and Cressida* Time the Chorus comes 'not in confidence / Of author's pen or actor's voice'. Nor does he convey either the dramatist's politic self-depreciation— e.g.

> Thus far, with rough and all-unable pen
> Our bending author hath pursued the story—

or the players' conventional apologies—as in

> But pardon, gentles all,
> The flat unraised spirits that hath dar'd
> On this unworthy scaffold. . . .

He speaks only on his own behalf. With the authority of the most venerable antiquity—

> Let me pass
> The same I am, ere ancient'st order was,
> Or what is now receiv'd—

he takes it on himself to slide over sixteen years, without touching on what happened in the interval. If it is not in accordance with dramatic law or custom to do this, he says, no serious objection should be raised ('Impute it not a crime / To me'), since both law and custom are at the mercy of time, which existed long before either. In this way Shakespeare is enabled to maintain unbroken the continuity of artistic authority which is the dramatist's privilege within the limits of his play, but which the use of conventional intervening chorus can well interrupt by acknowledging other authorities and other standards.

There was no necessity for him to introduce a chorus at all at this point, for later, in IV, ii, he uses other, more specifically dramatic, means to give much the same narrative information as Time gives

us here. But what counts in this place is the immediacy and vivid-
ness of the impact.[1] The arresting, eye-catching mode of presentation, unique in the play, interrupting the action and abruptly
involving a complete change of mood and style, corresponds in
its instantaneous effect upon the audience to the effect of the time
shift itself. Its use is both prudent and mannerly. It shows at once
that the dramatist is concerned not only to spare the spectator
possible confusion or embarrassment, but also to anticipate (or at
least not to pass over unrecognized) his critical objections.

Shakespeare, unlike Jonson, is not a man to cross critical
swords in the theatre, and the wit of his device for securing the
willing suspension of disagreement for the moment is quite
brilliant. For with solemn levity he refers the question of the unity
of time to the arbitration of Time himself. Time civilly admits that
sixteen years is a 'wide gap', but exercising his power to 'plant and
o'erwhelm' convention announces a *fait accompli*.

II

So, with the underlying implication that romance has its own rules,
the long lapse of time is asserted and plausibly placed beyond
critical dispute, the patient co-operation of the audience being
assumed (15). But what of the agency through which this has been
brought about? Does not Time the Chorus seem to have been
foisted upon the play? Can he not be made a more authentic part
of the construction, built into it more securely?

Not without robbing the play of dramatic power. In *Pericles*,
which is essentially a series of dramatized episodes, Gower is
constantly at hand to preserve narrative continuity, filling in gaps
in the story between the episodes (IV, iv, 8). No fuss needs to be
made over the great gap of time that separates the third and fourth

[1] As Pafford notes (p. xxxi), Greene bridges the time gap by touching
briefly on Fawnia's childhood, and then on her early girlhood when she was
seven and ten: in half a page she has reached the age of sixteen. Shakespeare
does no such thing: *The Winter's Tale* is not like *Pericles* a chronicle play. He
emphasizes the temporal gap, and in so doing achieves coherence of dramatic
effect, for the suddenness of its presentation harmonizes with the suddenness
of Leontes' possession at the beginning of the play and with the surprise of
Hermione's restoration at the end.

acts of that play: where there are many lesser gaps this one makes no special impact; and they are all filled up. Gower plays the interim: the more episodic the play the more firmly he establishes his right to be there.

In introducing Time the Chorus into *The Winter's Tale*, on the other hand, Shakespeare is careful not to give him any extra-dramatic narrative function. If Time breaks with law in sliding over sixteen years he breaks with custom in leaving 'the growth untried / Of that wide gap'. Any such material, Time implies, would simply not be relevant. What is to the dramatist's purpose lies on either side of the gap. The 'growth' of what happens in between is of no account: it is what developed in those sixteen years, not the steps in its development, that concerns the later stages of the play. So, besides stifling critical objections, Time is there simply to pass smoothly ('slide') from one side of the gap to the other.[1]

But if so, why does he ask us to imagine that *he* is in Bohemia (21)? (Chorus in *Henry V* would ask us to imagine that *we* were there.) Why does it matter *where* he is? With Leontes, shut up with his grief, time presumably stands still; and therefore, it seems,

[1] That criticism, like Time, should leave the growth of the wide gap untried is a corollary that has not commonly been drawn. The events of *The Winter's Tale* do not, like those of *Pericles*, 'occupy' over sixteen years (cf. E. C. Pettet, p. 175). It is in contrast a compact, concentrated play. Again, Time tells us something of Leontes, Florizel and Perdita, but not of Hermione or Paulina. We are as far as possible to slide over thoughts of them. 'When and by whom was the plan to conceal Hermione made? How could Hermione have been concealed? These and similar matters cannot occur to an audience. *They cannot exist when the play is performed* and therefore do not arise in our appreciation of it' (Pafford, p. li). The point is so crucial that I have italicized the essential part; for that is precisely what Time is saying.

But to stifle all such speculation is perhaps more than can be expected. Even Pafford allows himself to refer, like Mrs. Jameson (ii, 22) and Bethell (pp. 75, 95), to Hermione's 'religious retreat' (pp. xlv, lxxiv), and to glance at Paulina's stage-managing everything throughout the time gap, acting a lie for sixteen years (pp. lxxv, lxxix)—only to remind us, of course, that these are matters 'that we are not meant to scrutinize'. As we shall see, while not encouraging such speculation Shakespeare does make some provision for it. But, again as we shall see, it would be quite improper for us to couple with it anything in the nature of moral obloquy—to talk, for instance, as has been done, of 'the unrelenting behaviour of Hermione, a generous and tender-hearted woman, in pretending to be dead for sixteen long years in order to punish a thoroughly chastened and repentant husband'.

Time goes to Bohemia. But why this witty fancy? What more has Time to do with the play than to tell us of the passing of time? The next line tells us: '*I* mentioned a son o' th' king's'—in Act I. We are to think of Time as the story-teller—not like Gower, supplying bits of narrative here and there, but unfolding the story scene by scene as it is performed by the actors. It is '*my* tale' —a winter's tale seeming stale to the passing fashion of the moment (13)—'*my* scene', whose characters and relationships have developed in the course of time (16). Leaving Leontes grieving, Time is now, we are to imagine, in Bohemia; he names the king's son, whom he mentioned in a previous act, and hastens 'To speak of Perdita' (who is 'Time's news') in the coming act. She

> And what to her adheres, which follows after,
> Is th'argument of Time.

Time the Chorus appears this once: the idea that the play is his story acted out as he tells it is confined to this place. This is a neat and pleasant fancy worked out in harmony with the mood of easy good humour in which the whole passage is written. Has it a value outside itself? It is turned to advantage in two ways. First, it playfully justifies Time's intrusion as Chorus, giving him for the moment a perfect right to appear in the play. Secondly, it stimulates a state of expectancy in the audience regarding Perdita and her affairs, spending a number of lines elaborately not giving anything away. These forthcoming delights Time as story-teller can decently puff in terms which the author might hesitate to use if speaking *in propria persona*:

> Of this allow,
> If ever you have spent time worse ere now;
> If never, yet that Time himself doth say,
> He wishes earnestly you never may.

III

In Rosalind's view, though a good play may need no epilogue, yet good plays prove the better by the help of good epilogues. So with Time the Chorus in this play. He is not necessary, but his presence improves the play. Unheralded, his entrance is the more remarkable: no other chorus figure in Shakespeare makes his appearance in the course of the play without having been introduced at the beginning.

As we have just seen, his functions are two:

(1) To draw attention to the time gap, without apology: to establish it as an agreed convention of this play.
(2) To place emphasis on Perdita.

(1) It may be said that the time gap is sufficiently remarkable in itself, that it obtrudes itself, terminating an unusually close-knit succession of events, and transferring attention to other, contrasting interests. That is so: the time gap will in any case draw attention to itself—and be received perhaps with perplexity or derision. Those responses must be anticipated and corrected; but the time gap is not to be palliated or excused, but rather proclaimed, for it is a fundamental feature of the plot, part of the design, essential to Leontes, essential to Perdita, and through them, essential to Hermione.

(2) Perdita's fate and its far-reaching implications have been the centre of interest in three scenes, not to mention the oracle. Her story, though secondary, is vital, and in preparing the dénouement the fourth act develops it. But not at once. She was a young baby in the last scene, and even though sixteen years have officially passed we shall need a scene or two to get used to that idea before we see her grown to young womanhood. Hence the puff, the enticingly casual linking of her name with Florizel's, the assurance that she will be worth waiting for.[1]

---

[1] It is not impossible that the idea of Time's address grew out of Greene's transitionary sentence:

But leaving him [Pandosto] to his dolorous passions, at last let us come to show the tragical discourse of the young infant [Fawnia].

For Time certainly adapts the sentence in the course of his speech. It is the grown-up Perdita that matters in the play, not the stages in her growth; so for Shakespeare, causing Time to slide over sixteen years, Greene's sentence resolves itself into this:

But leaving him to his dolorous passions, at last let us come to show the comical discourse of the young woman.

That is to say:

> Leontes leaving,
> Th' effects of his fond jealousies so grieving

Scene Two

I

Shakespeare took particular pains with the structure of this play, and not least with the opening scenes of the acts. It is a pity, then, that the speech of Time the Chorus is labelled Scene i: no corresponding speech in Shakespeare is so labelled. The true opening of Act IV is the scene between Polixenes and Camillo. Here the action starts afresh after a lapse of sixteen years and harks back at once to the beginning of the play. In form it is identical with the first scene of all—a dialogue between two persons in courtly prose, the only other in the play. Camillo is again one of the speakers. With the other speaker, Polixenes, he was in urgent talk when we last saw them. As the scene opens Camillo has just renewed his request to return home to Sicilia. He is dissuaded. This reminds us of the start of all the trouble, when Polixenes wanted to return home to Bohemia, was dissuaded by Hermione, and soon had to run for his life with Camillo. Now the spiritual climate has changed. Camillo is anxious to go back to 'the penitent king, my master' (6). Leontes, whom Time the Chorus spoke of as shut up with his grief, has now stirred himself, has sent for Camillo and reconciled himself with Polixenes (23). These things he resolved to do sixteen years before in the first flush of his repentance. The fact that he has done so now combines the effect of the foreshortening of time with the suggestion of spiritual growth in Leontes: he has not made these approaches without due deliberation: at last he may be worthy that Polixenes should call him brother (24), and to have his counsellor, his priest-like confessor, back with him. Thus at the earliest moment we are assured that though time and place have changed Leontes is by no means lost to sight. The unity of the play is unimpaired. His sorrows are still fresh, but they may not be incapable of alleviation (7).

> That he shuts up himself, imagine me
> ... that I now ...
> with speed so pace
> To speak of Perdita, now grown in grace
> Equal with won'dring.

The plot can now be advanced a little, as Polixenes and Camillo, preparing the ground for the fourth scene, talk of spies and disguising, because of their fears of what Florizel may be up to. This new character—or rather, talk of him—emerges out of the carefully prepared links with the past, and indeed, in reminding us of Mamillius, is shown as such a link himself:

> Of that fatal country, Sicilia, prithee speak no more; whose very naming punishes me with the remembrance of the penitent (as thou call'st him) and reconciled king, my brother; whose loss of his most precious queen and children are even now to be afresh lamented. Say to me, when sawest thou the Prince Florizel, my son? Kings are no less unhappy, their issue not being gracious [as Polixenes fears Florizel is not], than they are in losing them when they have approved their virtues [as Leontes lost Mamillius].   (20)

Florizel, we learn, is seldom from the house of a most homely shepherd—rich, with a daughter of most rare note. We have already met this shepherd (in the last scene, albeit sixteen years ago), and will recognize him as another link with the past when we meet him again.

II

This is a gentle and highly effective way of accommodating the audience to the lapse of sixteen years—very different from abruptly making 'a child, now swaddl'd, to proceed / Man'. The technique is at once simple and subtle. It is *a long time* (two whole eventful acts) since Polixenes and Camillo were last before us. As we can see, they are older looking, and, as Polixenes puts it, 'punished' by the recollection of Leontes' lamentable losses. They themselves, that is to say, are the embodiment of time and its effects, and being an organic part of the plot they can, as Time the Chorus (a *deus ex tempore* in comparison) cannot, stand behind the forthcoming action as a means of contrast and guidance. Further, this technique prepares the way for our reception of Leontes in Act V. He has by then been off the stage for *a long time*—a whole act—during which much has happened. There has been a scene of considerable length and beauty, inducing a change of heart in the audience. Sixteen years before, 'A thousand knees / Ten thousand years

77

together' could not move the gods to look towards Leontes. But after Act IV the audience will be prepared to forgive the man; and it is the forgiveness of the audience that is dramatically required. As far as concerns the purgation of Leontes, then, the long fourth act stands for the time lapse of sixteen years, his spiritual regeneration, his rebirth.

Scene Three

I

Having shown the new act as closely related to what has passed, Shakespeare now introduces a new character quite unrelated to anything that has passed. We have been led to expect two other new characters, but not Autolycus: he is completely unexpected. He bursts upon the play unannounced, altering its tone, its point of view, enlarging its scope, at least for a time. He enters singing: hitherto we have had little to sing about. A sad tale's best for winter; but he sings of spring and summer. Possessing the style, assurance, independence and ready wit of an allowed jester, he compels excited and admiring attention in a way impossible for the *mere* ragged rogue and vagabond listed in the First Folio and described in Simon Forman's account of the play.

This scene intervenes not just so that Polixenes and Camillo may be abruptly replaced by actions and attitudes entirely at variance with theirs, but unobtrusively to enable the sheep-shearing scene to begin without preliminaries, and thus to give Florizel and Perdita a flying start. If Autolycus is to be there as the focus of interest in ballads and singing, it is well that he should explain himself to us beforehand; and he must have the means of learning that the event is to take place.[1] This he does by eavesdropping in the exercise of his profession of cony-catching—only one of his professions, of course, for he is a regular Pooh-Bah of knavery.

Autolycus is a thoroughgoing scoundrel. At the moment when

---

[1] Greene's 'meeting of all the farmers' daughters' becomes in Shakespeare's hands a sheep-shearing feast, with singing and dancing, at which the presence of a ballad-pedlar is appropriate.

the Clown is doing him a good turn he robs him. But that, of course, is not the emphasis, for his thievery is all the best of fun. He cheats and filches with the greatest good humour in the world. For he does but jest, pilfer in jest. Half the time he is exchanging winks with the audience. We are on terms with him: we are his ally. *He* is no thief, only a stage thief. So we can afford to give our censorious faculties a holiday. He is one of those vagrants whom Elizabethan law tried to bring under its rule to their extirpation, but whose arrival at a village fair might be a nine-days' wonder— one whose indifference to settled ways excites the secret envy and admiration of more timorous souls. Most of us have a soft place in our hearts for his like—'I'm off with the raggle-taggle gypsies, O!'—since he stands for the spot of the Old Adam needed to save men—from priggishness.

II

The baby turned marriageable maiden within the same play (and *a fortiori* within a scene or two) was a familiar critical crux of romantic plays: 'how absurd it is in sence', said Sidney (I, 197), 'euen sence may imagine'. Against that jolting sensation the delightful shock of Autolycus's entrance may by anticipation act as a shock-absorber—not only blunting by familiarity sensitiveness to later shock, but sharpening by delightful experience further expectation of delight.

The way is being prepared, then, for Florizel and Perdita. Their welcome will be enhanced by the slight delay. Scene ii, with the pattern of the play in view, asserted continuity with the world of Leontes. Following at once, Florizel and Perdita might have started at a disadvantage, having to create a sense of their own relevance and validity. The intervening scene goes some distance towards doing that for them, by widening the scope, extending the sympathetic responses of the audience. To pass at once from Polixenes and Camillo about to spy on the young people to the accomplishment of their purpose would concentrate attention too exclusively upon the story content, narrowing the imaginative and symbolic range. The love of Florizel and Perdita is important, of course, but it gains in importance when seen as an expression

79

of youth in general. The virility of youth, its power to go its own way, its faith in the outcome, these are leading motives in the next scene. Autolycus prepares the way. He after his fashion is a spokesman of youth, its heedlessness of restraint, its impulsiveness and wandering gaiety. He stands for the 'kingly' state of youth in most unkingly circumstances, taking what it can get, as of right. He is a thief and Florizel an honest man; he is heartless and promiscuous, a pragmatist, Florizel constant, a man of honour and principle. But they are both young: full-blooded, forthright and positive. 'Apprehend / Nothing but jollity', 'And let's be red with mirth', Florizel is to say. Autolycus sings 'A merry heart goes all the day', and 'the red blood reigns in the winter's pale'.[1]

III

The Clown is a link between past and future: we met him in the last act and shall meet him again, we learn, at the sheep-shearing feast. But he is not much more than a physical link. In function he is here a warm-hearted, soft-headed, easy gull, displaying the incomparably superior abilities of Autolycus. He is also a source of information. Through him we learn of the coming festivities, of his supposed sister's being mistress of the feast, and of the excellence of the singing that is to come. To crown our expectation of further pleasure Autolycus resolves to be there himself.

Scene Four

I

In presenting Florizel and Perdita Shakespeare makes a transparently deliberate attempt upon us. They start the scene, Florizel talking to Perdita:

> These your unusual weeds, to each part of you
> Do give a life: no shepherdess, but Flora
> Peering in April's front. This your sheep-shearing

[1] There is even an anticipatory link with Perdita (iv, 118) in the opening words of his song: 'When daffodils being to peer'.

Is as a meeting of the petty gods
And you the queen on't.[1]

With her usual weeds Perdita has laid aside the humdrum. She is transfigured; the sheep-shearing is transfigured. Pastoral, itself ideal, is further idealized, with due decorum: if in their looks Perdita and the rest resemble godhead, the order of godhead suggested ('petty gods') is the order proper to pastoral association.

The case of Florizel is different: he is a prince stooping to rusticity, his 'high self obscur'd / With a swain's wearing'. But this does not conflict with the main tenor: rather it emphasizes it. For it throws Perdita into prominence and ensures that her restraint, good sense and womanly feeling shall make a full contribution to the scene. Again, the fact of his disguise harmonizes with the prevailing tone, for everyone is dressed up: no one is what he seems. Besides Perdita and Florizel, Polixenes and Camillo are in disguise, the rustics are in their best attire, and Autolycus is pretending not to be Autolycus (wearing a 'pedlar's excrement'). Later in the scene Florizel and Perdita again disliken 'The truth of [their] own seeming'. Florizel and Autolycus exchange clothes. Clearly Florizel's costume ('a swain's wearing') is stylized, for it makes Autolycus pass for a gentleman even among gentlemen. And if Perdita is 'Most goddess-like prank'd up' (10), he can jestingly find godlike example for taking the likeness of 'a poor humble swain'—no less an example than that of 'the fire-rob'd god, / Golden Apollo', the tutelary god of the action of the play, and nowhere more obviously so than in this scene, a scene

[1] In *Pandosto*, to protect her from the sun, Fawnia wears a garland of boughs and flowers, 'which attire became her so gallantly as she seemed to be the goddess Flora herself for beauty' (p. 202). Much of the effect is lost by making this her everyday costume. By limiting to a special occasion Perdita's likeness to the goddess of spring Shakespeare gives it point and emphasis.

The special occasion corresponds, as we have noted, to the 'meeting of all the farmers' daughters in Sicilia', with sports and homely pastimes, which comes rather later in *Pandosto* (p. 204). For this Fawnia puts on her best clothes: she is 'bidden as the mistress of the feast'. The nature of the 'meeting' demands radical alteration at the dramatist's hands, however: Greene's is a 'hen' party.

It is after this party that Dorastus first meets Fawnia, as she returns home with another girl. Shakespeare gets to the heart of the matter without preliminaries: Florizel and Perdita have already come to an understanding when they meet at the sheep-shearing (50). This is no *Romeo and Juliet*.

outstanding even in Shakespeare for its poetical and visual beauty.[1]

Perdita has that clearness of judgement with which Shakespeare customarily endows his girl-lovers: and with it she charmingly tempers her loyal acceptance of Florizel's leadership. She has an unfailing sense of the fitness of things. At once she demurs at

---

[1] Florizel's speech about the gods opens with a snatch of *Pandosto* turned to humour and to poetry. The speech goes thus:

> Apprehend
> Nothing but jollity. The gods themselves,
> Humbling their deities to love, have taken
> The shapes of beasts upon them: Jupiter
> Became a bull, and bellow'd; the green Neptune
> A ram, and bleated; and the fire-rob'd god,
> Golden Apollo, a poor humble swain,
> As I seem now. Their transformations
> Were never for a piece of beauty rarer,
> Nor in a way so chaste, since my desires
> Run not before mine honour, nor my lusts
> Burn hotter than my faith. (24)

In *Pandosto* Fawnia has told Dorastus that she can love him 'when Dorastus becomes a shepherd' (p. 209). So, struggling with the indignity of it he puts on shepherd's robes, and before presenting himself to her again, seeks consolation in the thought:

shame not at thy shepherd's weed. The heavenly gods have sometime earthly thoughts. Neptune became a ram, Jupiter a bull, Apollo a shepherd: they gods, and yet in love; and thou a man appointed to love. (p. 210)

That passage has often been noted in this connexion, but not, I think, another—an earlier reflection of Dorastus's—which Shakespeare associates with it:

The gods above disdain not to love women beneath. Phoebus liked Sibylla, Jupiter Io, and why not I then Fawnia? one something inferior to these in birth, but far superior to them in beauty, born to be a shepherd, but worthy to be a goddess.

However that may be, she is still greatly below Dorastus in rank; and he continues in a spirit of retraction:

Ah, Dorastus, wilt thou so forget thyself as to suffer affection to suppress wisdom, and love to violate thine honour? (p. 206)

In Shakespeare's transformation of all this, the lover is freed from any suspicion of arrogance, or distrust of love. He is gay and unassuming, his own man, not troubled by thoughts of rank, or fear of displeasing his father by rash surrender to unworthy affection. (On this see further in Appendix I D.) More important, Florizel's symbolic humility exalts him, likening him to Golden Apollo; if Perdita, like Fawnia, is more beautiful than a goddess the comparison leads Florizel to think of himself in his love as more honourable and faithful than the gods (who in contrast by lustful love 'violate their honour').

Florizel's inversion of order in his choice of costumes for them, but she sees how ill it would become her sex and station to chide at his 'extremes', and, recognizing that the custom of the feast involves such 'folly', she checks her instinctive blushes at its impropriety. The inequality of their rank troubles her more, not because she feels herself unworthy of Florizel, but because it must incline the king against their marriage. It is plain that if she had felt herself unworthy her common sense would itself have opposed all thoughts of the match. This we see from the uncompromising conservatism of her views on the practice of grafting 'A gentler scion to the wildest stock' (93, 99).[1] Her sense of her own worth is unconscious not expressed: her noble birth proclaims itself in her delicacy of taste and feeling:

> Nothing she does or seems
> But smacks of something greater than herself,
> Too noble for this place. (157)

Consciously she sees her royal lover's abilities as greatly exceeding her own, and finds equality only in the assumption that his love is as pure as hers is:

> I cannot speak
> So well, nothing so well, no, nor mean better:
> By th' pattern of mine own thoughts I cut out
> The purity of his.

This is lover's logic. Her womanly prudence is in abeyance because its scruples have been satisfied:

> but that your youth
> And the true blood which peepeth fairly through't
> Do plainly give you out an unstain'd shepherd,
> With wisdom I might fear, my Doricles,
> You woo'd me the false way. (147)

So her conservative nature reconciles itself with the strongest romantic impulses. She shows the quiet confidence in her own

[1] Pafford (p. 169) quotes the passages from Florio's Montaigne and Puttenham's *Arte of English Poesie* which set forth Perdita's and Polixenes' positions in the Art *versus* Nature debate. This debate was a commonplace, but there is good reason for thinking that Shakespeare had these particular passages in mind here. Quite possibly he looked them over with the statue scene in view, for there, as Kermode (p. xxxv) and Lawlor (p. 112) remark, art becomes nature; but it is here not there that he makes special use of them.

judgement which it is Ophelia's misfortune to lack. Her reason puts aside the normal counsel of reason to look before you leap, not to judge by appearances, and accepts instead the counsel of love to take a chance, to judge as one would be judged oneself, to trust in the honour of one's lover. Thus her sense of the fitness of things carries her towards the democratic conclusion:

> once or twice
> I was about to speak, and tell him plainly,
> The selfsame sun that shines upon his court
> Hides not his visage from our cottage, but
> Looks on alike. (443)

But, poised between the two extremes, she is swayed by her native conservatism and keeps silence. Heart-broken she sees that she and Florizel must part, and the sooner the better. Her hopes have been but a dream: now she will 'queen it no inch farther' (450).

Miranda's enthusiastic delight in the 'brave new world' is balanced by Prospero's experience—''Tis new to thee'. But in *The Winter's Tale* Perdita's generous trust has the last word. Camillo speaks of the fragility of love:

> Prosperity's the very bond of love,
> Whose fresh complexion and whose heart together
> Affliction alters. (574)

'One of these is true,' she replies,

> I think affliction may subdue the cheek
> But not take in the mind;[1]

and, turning to Florizel, who delightedly concurs, Camillo pays handsome tribute to this as a statement of right royal wisdom:

Camillo   Yea? say you so?
There shall not, at your father's house, these seven years
Be born another such.
Florizel   My good Camillo,
She is as forward of her breeding as
She is i' th' rear 'our birth.

---

[1] The thought and military image come from *Pandosto*, where Fawnia, resisting the king's libidinous advances, says: 'Pandosto, the body is subject to victories, but the mind not to be subdued by conquest' (p. 221). Shakespeare's originality lies in his use of the thought to impress Camillo with Perdita's innate nobility of mind.

It is characteristic of Perdita that in her affirmation of faith she thinks of love as of the mind, as based in reason.

As Perdita is an ideal expression of maidenhood, so Florizel is a heightened representation of an honourable young man in love. To him his lady's every action is quintessential (135). His feelings are transparently honourable: his 'true blood' peeps 'fairly' through his youth. This, we are to understand, is the essential thing. Like the amorous gods he may appear to invert degree, but unlike them he puts honour and faith before desire (33). He may fly in the face of fact—as Perdita the realist cannot do (35)—of parental authority, inheritance, fate itself. The old saw 'who shall give a lover any law?' may be implicit in Florizel's arguments; but he softens its core of selfishness—'Ech man for him-self, ther is non other'—by making the loss of individuality through love necessary to attain the ideal of 'knowing oneself':

> Or I'll be thine, my fair,
> Or not my father's. For I cannot be
> Mine own, nor anything to any, if
> I be not thine. To this I am most constant,
> Though destiny say no. (42)

II

Florizel and Perdita are given fifty lines alone together to establish the tone of the scene. Then Polixenes, Camillo and the Old Shepherd join them with others for the merry-making, and these form the background against which youth is set. Polixenes' disguise makes him seem as old as Camillo (78, 357, 362, 405), so that age and youth are sharply contrasted in spite of Perdita's tact in offering to the old 'flowers / Of middle summer' (106). A wind of March in such a gathering, Polixenes is 'taken' with Perdita's beauty. While pumping the Old Shepherd, he nevertheless enters into the spirit of the event as becomes an honoured guest, and will not allow his host to cut short the entertainment on his account (336). When he judges that the time has come to part the lovers he comes forward in a mood of urbane levity, shared by Camillo (379), which he maintains for a time even when it appears that Florizel expects them then and there to witness and hence validate the union (391). Florizel speaks unfeelingly of his father to the Old Shepherd (388) and to the disguised Polixenes:

Polixenes Have you a father? . . .
            Knows he of this?
Florizel   He neither does nor shall.   (393)

Yet Polixenes is mild, reasonable and touching in his appeal to his headstrong son:

> By my white beard,
> You offer him, if this be so, a wrong
> Something unfilial: reason my son
> Should choose himself a wife, but as good reason
> The father, all whose joy is nothing else
> But fair posterity, should hold some counsel
> In such a business.   (405)

This mildness is designed to heighten the surprise of his sudden fury. The passage continues:

Polixenes   Let him know't.
Florizel   He shall not.
Polixenes   Prithee, let him.
Florizel   No, he must not.
Shepherd   Let him, my son: he shall not need to grieve
            At knowing of thy choice.
Florizel   Come, come, he must not.
            Mark our contract.

'Mark your divorce, young sir', cries Polixenes, throwing off his disguise. It is a splendidly theatrical moment, briefly comparable with Ferdinand's 'Die then, quickly'. But Polixenes has been driven to it by Florizel's persistence. He *must* unmask at this point, *must* play the heavy father.

Conditional disinheritance (in the heat of the moment) we can understand. But why

> I'll have thy beauty scratch'd with briers and made
> More homely than thy state

to Perdita? And why 'hanging' for the Old Shepherd, who far from being a traitor has just supported Polixenes in urging Florizel to tell his father of his choice? These sentences may seem fantastic—and no less so the sudden unsolicited suspension of their enforcement (433)—so extravagant that we can hardly take

86

them seriously; and that is one aspect of the situation. But it is not the only one. The other is that this is tyranny and injustice at their worst. The Old Shepherd's reading of his wrongs may indeed almost seem a correlative in miniature at the bucolic level of Hermione's concern about the threat to her honour:

> 'Tis a derivative from me to mine,
> And only that I stand for.

For the Old Shepherd is the repository of the good old pieties. 'I'll take it up for pity', he said during the storm; and lately he has been holding up his old dead wife as a model of how unsparing a hostess should be in her attention to her guests, and, ironically, urging Perdita particularly to welcome their unknown friends (Polixenes and Camillo), 'for it is / A way to make us better friends, more known' (65). Now Polixenes has even regretted that by hanging the Old Shepherd he could 'But shorten [his] life one week' (423). It is not only the old man, however, who has been abused ('old traitor,' 'hanging'), but through him a way of life, a tradition.

> You have undone a man of fourscore three,
> That thought to fill his grave in quiet: yea,
> To die upon the bed my father died,
> To lie close by his honest bones: but now
> Some hangman must put on my shroud and lay me
> Where no priest shovels-in dust. O cursed wretch,
> That knew'st this was the prince, and wouldst adventure
> To mingle faith with him? Undone! Undone!
> If I might die within this hour, I have liv'd
> To die when I desire.   (453)

The corresponding scene in Greene occurs later on in the story and directly concerns Pandosto.[1] Egistus sends an embassage asking him to have Fawnia, the old shepherd Porrus, and Dorastus's servant, old Capnio, put to death. Pandosto willingly condemns them, but considering Capnio a traitor he sentences him not to easy death but to have his eyes put out and continually to 'grind

---

[1] It is earlier anticipated, however, by Fawnia's fears when she and her sweetheart plight their troth and Dorastus determines that they shall go to Italy. 'This device was greatly praised of Fawnia, for she feared if the king his father should but hear of the contract, that his fury would be such as no less than death would stand for payment' (p. 212).

87

in a mill like a brute beast'. The sentences are not carried out as Porrus thereupon speaks up and Fawnia's parentage is revealed. Shakespeare rejects the gratuitous cruelty of Capnio's sentence, but introduces a petty barbarity (scratching with briers) in similarly wanton vein.[1] The chief point that emerges from the comparison, however, is that he transfers to Polixenes Pandosto's intended tyrannies, for which Egistus, Polixenes' counterpart, is morally responsible. Shakespeare uses them to afford fleeting but impressive parallels with Leontes in the earlier part of the play, reminding us of his rage, his sudden cruelties, his vacillation. In both cases the pleasing affirmation of the joy of parenthood (e.g. 409) sharpens the shock of what immediately follows. There is corresponding extravagance of mood. The relation between this and past scenes is of course only that of shadow to substance, of threat to fulfilment. Yet though the sentences (422, 426) are suspended (434) as suddenly as they are imposed, their effect, as we have seen from the Old Shepherd's speech, is by no means shadowy. Just as Leontes' rage and cruelty caused Polixenes and Camillo to run for their lives and his infant daughter to be cast out and put to sea, so now both the kings' children will have to fly—she at the risk of cruel death (441), he of disinheritance (430). And they would be 'the slaves of chance, and flies / Of every wind that blows', were it not, once more, for the kindly guidance of age. The parallelism produces a sense not only of unity in diversity but also of controlling purpose behind the seemingly haphazard and accidental.

III

The staginess of Polixenes' fury carries with it two conveniently stagy consequences: he orders Florizel to follow him to the court but does not wait to see that he does so, and he forgets to take

---

[1] Later in the scene (785) Autolycus, to frighten the Clown into his power, alludes with lofty gaiety to the manner of Ambrogiuolo's death in Boccaccio (*Decameron* ii, 9; J. M. Nosworthy, p. xxi), embroidering it freely. Possibly it was here in connexion with Polixenes' threats, while he was momentarily occupied with bizarre tortures, that Shakespeare remembered that horrible punishment—so grotesque that, suitably elaborated, he found burlesque use for it in the broad comedy of the concluding passage of the scene.

Camillo with him. Both therefore remain behind; and Perdita will stay with them for their vital scene together, ending with the elopement. First, however, the objects of the king's displeasure tell in turn how they have taken his outburst. After Perdita's speech, brave but hopeless, Camillo turns to the Old Shepherd saying

> Why, how now, father!
> Speak ere thou diest. (451)

He can hardly have failed to understand that the sentences have been revoked. He can hardly be so cruel as deliberately to deceive the Old Shepherd, whether in jest or in earnest, into thinking that the sentence of hanging still stands. The only remaining possibility is unseasonable bluff heartiness: 'Hi, there, old fellow, you *are* looking pretty ghastly. Let's hear what you have to say before you drop dead'.

It has suddenly been revealed to this aged man in quick succession that the guest he has been entertaining is no less a person than the king (418), that Perdita's sweetheart, whom he has been encouraging, is the prince (419), that he is himself condemned to be hanged as a traitor (421), and that Perdita knew all the time that the so-called Doricles was Florizel (424). That was the crowning shock. 'O, my heart!' he ejaculated; and the enormity of it still preys on his mind thirty lines later:

> O cursed wretch,
> That knew'st this was the prince, and wouldst adventure
> To mingle faith with him! Undone, undone! (459)

No wonder Camillo thinks he looks like death. No wonder he has been too dazed to understand that his sentence has been revoked; and naturally, therefore, when Camillo jolts him in his misery he takes the king's friend's unfortunate choice of words as confirming his impression that 'Some hangman must put on my shroud . . .'. The supposed Doricles has 'undone' him (454); his supposed daughter has 'undone' him (459–61). All he can hope for now is to avoid a traitor's death by dying at once:

> If I might die within this hour, I have liv'd
> To die when I desire.

To the command, 'Speak ere thou diest' he has replied:

> I cannot speak, nor think,
> Nor dare to know, that which I know. (452)

Everything he has held most certain is now uncertain, he means: he cannot dare to make any affirmation, and so reasoning from known postulates, and therefore speech, are impossible for him. He goes on then to indicate the things he thought he knew and which have proved illusory: that Doricles and Perdita were to be trusted, and that he would die peacefully in the bed his father died in and would be buried near to him.[1]

That probably is all he is intended to mean. There is something more, of course, that he thinks he knows: that Perdita is not his daughter but, it would seem, the bastard issue of some noble liaison. This, as we must suppose, he is too dazed now to focus in the light of his general perplexity, and hence he certainly cannot speak it. But later in the scene this is what he will want to tell the king, so as to clear himself of blood relationship with Perdita, and hence of responsibility for her offence—later, as the plot requires, not now.[2]

IV

Probably the most significant part of the scene is the colloquy between Florizel and Camillo. Here Florizel splendidly expresses the heady self-determination of youth, its will to break down all barriers to secure its own object. That such proceeding is virtuous is an article of romantic faith, at least when exercised in the service of love.

Here Shakespeare gives that doctrine its head. A pair of lovers, by no means 'star-crossed', take matters into their own hands, and with much assistance from the old (Camillo has far greater

---

[1] The comma after 'dare to know' is probably rhetorical, and it is customary to omit it. Whether we do so or not, the meaning is essentially the same.

[2] In *Pandosto* Porrus's disclosures immediately follow the king's announcement of the sentences:

'Pandosto, and ye noble ambassadors of Sicilia, seeing without cause I am condemned to die, I am yet glad I have opportunity to disburden my conscience before my death. I will tell you as much as I know, and yet no more than is true. . . .' (pp. 223–4)

He speaks with assurance. He has long known that Fawnia's sweetheart is the prince; he has not been branded as a traitor; the bottom has not dropped out of his world: he is in full possession of his faculties.

power of direction than Friar Lawrence) help in the process of reconciliation, and yet live.[1] In the first movement of the play love was severed by jealousy, that is by betrayal of love; in the later part it is knit up by truth to love.

Florizel has two guides, his own faith and Camillo's reason. His faith receives the strongest possible statement. His intention to marry Perdita, he says,

> cannot fail but by
> The violation of my faith; and then
> Let nature crush the sides o' the earth together
> And mar the seeds within.   (477)

The similarity of the image to Lear's 'Crack nature's moulds, all germens spill at once' and Macbeth's 'Though the treasure / Of nature's germens tumble all together' has often been noticed. The tragic heroes speak as destroyers: that the seeds of life should be spilled is for them a thing to be desired or a matter of indifference. With Florizel it is very different. To him such a catastrophe is unthinkable—as unthinkable as that he should break his faith.

This is not the world of tragedy; yet such faith could well lead to tragedy. For it is headstrong, based on 'affection' and 'fancy' not reason; and it horrifies Camillo, the spokesman of reason.

Florizel From my succession wipe me, father; I
         Am heir to my affection.
Camillo   Be advis'd.
Florizel I am: and by my fancy. If my reason
         Will thereto be obedient, I have reason;
         If not, my senses, better pleas'd with madness,
         Do bid it welcome.   (481)

Here is an inversion of degree parallel, when considered abstractly, to that of Leontes, who allowed fancy which leads to madness to oversway his judgement; and Camillo is again at hand to protest to its royal victim against the monstrousness of it.

Florizel granted his disguised father's arguments about filial duty but overruled them in his own mind with 'some other

---

[1] Leontes and Hermione are the only characters in *The Winter's Tale* who speak of being star-crossed—Leontes when not himself, and Hermione looking forward in the same breath to a more favourable aspect of the heavens. At the end of the play Leontes, regenerate, talks of the 'heavens directing' the young people's affairs (I, ii, 201; II, i, 105; V, iii, 150).

reasons' which he kept to himself (412). Here he tells us what they
are. To Camillo's protest, 'This is desperate, sir', he replies

> So call it: but it does fulfil my vow;
> I needs must think it honesty. Camillo,
> Not for Bohemia, nor the pomp that may
> Be thereat glean'd: for all the sun sees, or
> The close earth wombs, or the profound seas hides
> In unknown fathoms, will I break my oath
> To this my fair belov'd.

He has a code of honour, the fitting code for a prince: 'To thine
own self be true'. He must keep his vow: Perdita's dignity cannot
fail but by the violation of his faith. The point is of special importance in its bearing on the first movement of the play. There Leontes, suddenly losing faith in his beloved, calumniated her honour.
Here Florizel's faith in himself and in Perdita, his identification of
his own honour with hers, are so excitingly proclaimed that we
must believe that he would stand though Leontes fell. The strength
of his faith and honour seems to redress the balance and to make
reparation for Leontes' weakness and consequent crime.

Florizel's subjection to fancy is a noble thing; Leontes' was
wholly despicable. Nevertheless, lacking the control of reason,
Florizel is dangerously insecure. This is symbolized by his intention to 'put to sea / With her whom here I cannot hold on shore'
(499); and his insecurity is emphasized by Camillo's remark:

> O my lord,
> I would your spirit were easier for advice,
> Or stonger for your need.

Such strength Camillo resolves to supply by offering the 'direction'
of reason—'if', he adds, smiling to himself,

> If your more ponderous and settled project
> May suffer alteration.   (524)

But Florizel of course has no ponderous or settled project.[1]

[1] In *Pandosto*, Dorastus's old servant Capnio agrees to help his master to
flee to Italy with Fawnia, 'seeing no persuasions could prevail to divert him
from his settled determination'. This, it seems, makes Shakespeare chuckle,
for such a 'determination' makes no sense: Italy has no relevance in the story.
A chance storm has to intervene to drive the fugitives to the shores of
Pandosto's country. Dorastus may think he has a settled project, but in fact
he is the slave of chance and needs—what Greene does not give him—the
direction of age.

He will act 'wildly', putting the blame for this on his father's unexpected intervention (539). Like any other slave of fancy, like Leontes 'a feather for each wind that blows', he professes himself and Perdita 'to be the slaves of chance, and flies / Of every wind that blows' (541).

Camillo's advice—

> A course more promising
> Than a wild dedication of yourselves
> To unpath'd waters, undream'd shores, most certain
> To miseries enough—   (566)

reminds us incidentally of what happened to Antigonus and might have happened to Perdita as a result of Leontes' evil action taken in the teeth of good advice. This is another turn of the screw tightening the connexion between this phase of the play and the first. But the primary concern of the passage is with the insecurity of youth, no matter how confident, courageous or honest it may be, and its dependence on the wisdom and benevolence of age. Camillo, 'Preserver of my father, now of me, / The medicine of our house' (587), will perform 'almost a miracle' (535), as Paulina, that other medicine and preserver, is yet to do for Perdita's. He who

> to the certain hazard
> Of all uncertainties, himself commended,
> No richer than his honour   (III, ii, 168)

now gives guidance to others who take the same course. But just as, in the opening act, in saving Polixenes he discovered in the king's enforced flight the means of finding a haven for himself, so here he makes Florizel's flight the opportunity of again getting what he wants for himself, to go home and see his former master (509). Thus the main plot, while in abeyance, is kept moving and kept in sight, and the minor plot is duly subordinated to it as a possible means of securing reconciliation, as Camillo prophesies (548).

V

Low comedy appropriately ends the scene, separating the romance of runaway lovers from the romance of long sorrows and regeneration. Autolycus, having brought the sheep shearing incident to a

93

profitable conclusion (596ff.), has been at hand profitably to further the elopement by being bustled into an unwontedly honest and minor—though of course knowing (639, 643)—part in that piece of trickery. Part of his profit has been the fancy dress ('a swain's wearing') that Florizel wore at the sheep shearing; and this costume he at once uses as a means of yet further profit by gulling the Old Shepherd and his son in the character of a great courtier. Now once more under the influence of the Clown (at least until Autolycus pockets up his pedlar's excrement), the Old Shepherd is no longer a figure of pathos. His grudge against the prince—

> O sir!
> You have undone a man of fourscore three,
> That thought to fill his grave in quiet—

is now expressed in quite different terms:

> I will tell the king all, every word, yea, and his son's pranks too; who, I may say, is no honest man, neither to his father nor to me, to go about to make me the king's brother-in-law. (699)

Autolycus too has moral scruples, but a different ethical philosophy:

> if I thought it were a piece of honesty to acquaint the king withal, I would not do't: I hold it the more knavery to conceal it; and therein am I constant to my profession. (680)

Hence his kidnapping of the rustics, required by the plot, will have a comic inevitability inherent in the logic of character and situation.

'If I had a mind to be honest', he says at the end (832), 'I see Fortune would not suffer me'; but if Fortune may be said, as in Greene's account, to have a hand in the affair, none of the participants is the slave of chance. The rustics are actively gullible; and Autolycus has a keen and constant eye (ear, hand, nose) to business (670, 683). They mistake him for a courtier (729), and actually thrust money upon him in their eagerness to be taken to the ship (805, 809, 823), but not without manipulation and prompting from Autolycus (717, 724, 769–97).

This little episode is beautifully contrived. The whole Bohemian section is set in a frame, its two ends answering one another. The section begins (III, iii, 59) near the sea with the finding of gold and the resolution to do good deeds on't. It ends here, likewise near

94

the sea-side (826), and with Autolycus 'courted now with a double occasion—gold [the same gold that was found with Perdita], and a means to do the prince my master good'. The rustics are in similar mood.

Clown   We are blest in this man, as I may say, even blest.
Shepherd   Let's before, as he bids us: he was provided to do us good.

At the time this seems laughably ironic, but not in the long run. As it turns out, Autolycus has done them good against his will, and if his hopes of employment under the prince fade, he can take service under them. They, accustomed to performing 'good deeds', will be his 'good masters' (V, ii, 124, 113, 174).

VI

Honesty and trust are the keynote of the second movement of the play—the justification of the romantic standpoint—and the philosophy of Autolycus pleasantly exposes the extreme idealism of such faith. Honesty, he shows, is a fool, and trust a very simple gentleman (596). Plainly the gods connive at knavery; and Fortune drops booties in his mouth (833): 'The prince himself is about a piece of iniquity, stealing away from his father with his clog at his heels' (678).

But even though the truth of this philosophy is thus tellingly demonstrated in Florizel's behaviour no less than in his own, Autolycus's 'realism' does not shake the validity in its context of the romantic idealism. Rather, his bantering tone bespeaks the triviality of his doctrine and the lighthearted nature of his adherence to it, and reinforces by contrast the memory of Florizel's earnest and settled conviction. Moreover his words belie him, for however much he may disparage honesty and trust he is at the end motivated like Camillo not only by self-seeking but also, surprising as it may seem, by benevolent loyalty: 'to do the prince my master good'.

An important function of the scene is to assert that faith and honour are the norm of gentlemanly conduct. Leontes offended against that code. His offence was isolated; it could spread no tragic infection; the code was not endangered, or the security of its operation. On the contrary, all others in Leontes' milieu were obedient to it. His was a private case, and needed private treatment. This scene does not symbolize his recovery; but it stands in place of it.

As we have observed, though Leontes is absent from the scene Polixenes and Camillo keep us in mind of his world. Before his exit Polixenes' sudden passion recalls Leontes'; and at their entrance the two 'reverend sirs', confronted by Perdita's spring, betoken the long winter of Leontes' penitence and regeneration during which remembrance and repentance keep 'seeming and savour' (73). In a manner, then, Leontes is through them bidden welcome to the sheep shearing, and its restorative alchemy is suggested by Perdita's happy word-play on rosemary (remembrance) and rue (repentance), the 'herb of grace':

> Grace and remembrance be to you both.

The words would befit Hermione, and while Perdita is no pale imitation of her mother, she has something of the strength of Hermione's gentleness, and for a moment, on a slighter scale, something of her spirited resignation (442). In a much-quoted passage she seems to suggest that love can as it were restore from the dead:

Perdita   O, these I lack,
    To make you garlands of, and my sweet friend,
    To strew him o'er and o'er!
Florizel   What? like a corse?
Perdita No, like a bank, for love to lie and play on:
    Not like a corse; or if—not to be buried,
    But quick, and in mine arms.

The scene shows the ability of faith and innocence led by the experience of age to work 'almost a miracle'. It shows a marriage being made not broken—self-made, not self-broken—and obstacles being surmounted by faith, not erected by blind suspicion and mistrust. Instead of Leontes, the slave of a destructive fancy, which is the negation of love and honour, we see Florizel deliberately subjecting himself to a creative fancy which is the expression of both. His confidence is infectious, his belief in the power of honour deeply impressive; but above all he gladly accepts the medicinable guidance of age in the person of Camillo, whose priest-like offices Leontes rejected. All this puts us in a state of preparedness for the discovery in the next act that a similar attitude has been induced in the already penitent Leontes, under the direction of the good Paulina.

Act Five   Scene One

I

To this act alone is there no preamble, involving minor characters, or moods soon to be disrupted. An oblique approach would, we can see, be out of place, even harmful perhaps. The action now returns to Leontes and his court, and the best thing is for it to do so directly.

In *Pandosto* the flight of Dorastus and Fawnia leads to:
(1) their arrival unexpectedly at Pandosto's court;
(2) the imprisonment of Dorastus; Pandosto's protracted attempt to seduce Fawnia;
(3) Egistus's dispatch of an embassage requesting the release of Dorastus and the death of his companions;
(4) the ensuing discovery of Fawnia's identity; the return to Egistus's country for the wedding; Pandosto's suicide.

Shakespeare gets to work on this series of events thus:

(1) After restoring Leontes and his affairs to the position of chief attention and concern, he uses the unexpected coming of the young people to display them as a beautiful and eminently desirable element in the world of the older generation, thus reaffirming the emphasis of the opening scene of the play. The announcement of their arrival varies the mood and tempo, and marks the first stage in a sequence of surprising incidents culminating in the statue scene.

(2) The noble king, now a model of courtliness and honour, can entertain no lustful thoughts, nor can he be discourteous in his reception of his wronged friend's son.

(3) Just as Leontes cannot be minded on his own account to imprison Florizel, so he cannot be called upon to put Florizel's companions to death. Foreseeing its unsuitability for this place, Shakespeare has thriftily recast this idea and used it in Act IV to cloud the pastoral world with shadows of past attitudes, and to motivate and justify the elopement.

Instead of sending an embassage, Egistus's counterpart in the play goes himself, urged on by Camillo, in instant pursuit of the runaway couple. Their arrival and Polixenes', following in quick succession, considerably enhance the atmosphere of turbulent excitement.[1]

(4) Polixenes' pursuit brings the two kings together personally, and so removes the need for further journeying within the limits of the play. It has the further happy consequence that the Old Shepherd can make his disclosures both to his own king (as he intended) and to the other (as the plot demands).

II

The long fourth act has kept Leontes out of sight and largely out of mind. It has dulled the edge of our hostility: our recollection of his impiety towards the gods, and more towards Hermione and his infant child, has been mellowed by time and by the warm feeling of what has passed since. We can therefore accept at once Cleomenes' opening statement that Leontes has redeemed his fault, that the heavens have now forgiven and forgotten it. The hopeless problem of dramatically representing long purgation has been obviated, and is replaced by its more plainly dramatic residual consequence: the king cannot forgive himself, and Paulina, a kind of conscience to him, rubs salt in his wounds (15). His last words to her, 'Come, and lead me / To these sorrows', join hands over the years with Cleomenes' initial assurance that he has 'perform'd / A saint-like sorrow'. The impression of unbroken continuity and efficacy in the process of spiritual restoration and probation is at once established; and its instrument, Paulina, is at hand, constantly nagging, putting him to the test, outraging Cleomenes with her apparently excessive and cruel zeal (23, 73, 75), reflecting in epitome what Leontes has been through all these years, and provoking him to show how completely his fiery spirit has been curbed and chastened (20, 68, 82, 118).

[1] It is noteworthy that Shakespeare does not introduce Polixenes in person at this point. He thus avoids representing two similar incidents one after the other, and gives extended prominence to Florizel and Perdita—and, what is more important, to Leontes' benevolence towards them. Polixenes' part is to swell the family rejoicings and complete the reunion, not that of angry parental intervention.

The first part of this scene, then (1–84), displays the completeness of Leontes' conversion, his piety, his acquiescence in righteous counsels. The display is given dramatic interest by being cast in the form of a conflict between Leontes and Paulina on one side and the courtiers on the other. This calls to mind the earlier scene (II, iii) in which Paulina in her virtue stood out alone against Leontes and in which he in his wrong-headedness stood out alone against the virtuous court. The settled strength of his humility now contrasts with the nervy uncertainty and fear, the essential weakness, of his former tyrannical state.

Apart from Leontes' regeneration the excellence of Hermione is the chief topic of this first section, linked with the possibility of the king's remarriage to get an heir. 'Her, and her virtues', 'she you kill'd', 'her that's gone' (17, 15, 35): Leontes and Paulina hardly need to name Hermione, so constantly is she in their thoughts, reminding Leontes of his crimes, as his first words show:

> Whilst I remember
> Her, and her virtues, I cannot forget
> My blemishes in them, and so think of
> The wrong I did myself: which was so much,
> That heirless it hath left my kingdom, and
> Destroyed the sweet'st companion that e'er man
> Bred his hopes out of. (6)

By making his thoughts run on his deprivation of issue Shakespeare seems to suggest that the long conjugal abstinence which was part of Leontes' spiritual exercise must soon draw to an end: 'so long', he said at its beginning—

> so long as nature
> Will bear up with this exercise, so long
> I daily vow to use it.

It is now possible to raise the question of his remarriage. This is more than a personal question: the courtiers take it up as a matter of urgent public concern (25, 28). Paulina, while quelling such talk, does not deny that it would be a holy work

> To bless the bed of majesty again
> With a sweet fellow to't:

what she says is that no one is so worthy of the office as Hermione ('her that's gone'). She does not say that the oracle will not be fulfilled, but that it is 'monstrous to our human reason' that it should; yet in spite of its seeming impossibility she has faith in its possibility (35).

> 'Tis your counsel,

she says to Cleomenes and Dion,

> My lord should to the heavens be contrary,
> Oppose against their wills. (44)

This argument is unanswerable. We remember what happened when Leontes opposed the heavens' wills in the last scene we saw him in. With quiet confidence she decides the matter: 'care not for issue; / The crown will find an heir' (46).

Thus under Paulina's authoritative direction the question of an heir is dropped, left to take care of itself, or rather left to the gods. But not the question of marriage.

> No more such wives; therefore, no wife: (56)

that is the logical conclusion, Leontes sees, of what Paulina is saying; and he is content:

> Fear thou no wife:
> I'll have no wife, Paulina. (68)

But that is not what she wants. What she gets him to swear is

> Never to marry, but by my free leave. (70)

And then she hints at the possibility that another wife might be found for him

> As like Hermione as is her picture— (74)

another that would be approved of by Hermione herself (80). Finally, this possibility she cryptically withdraws: 'That', she says,

> Shall be when your first queen's again in breath:
> Never till then.

What for the audience is the significance of all this? We are being put in possession of new information which is not perceived by the characters on the stage. Dramatic fact is changing before our eyes, or rather its nature is changing. It was an absolute fact that Hermione was irrevocably dead. Now it seems to be suggested that it is a contingent fact, dependent on the fulfilment of the oracle, which of course depends on the gods. In them Paulina has absolute faith, whatever human reason may say.

This is a mystery, and is communicated in mysterious terms:

> the gods
> Will have fulfilled their secret purposes:
> For has not the divine Apollo said,
> Is't not the tenor of his oracle,
> That King Leontes shall not have an heir
> Till his lost child be found? which that it shall
> Is all as monstrous to our human reason
> As my Antigonus to break his grave
> And come again to me; who, on my life,
> Did perish with the infant. (35)

The suggestion that a dead man should return from the grave, even though ostensibly mentioned as absurd, is of obvious dramatic importance in this place; and it is supported by the hypothesis, three times repeated, that Hermione herself might appear as a ghost:

Leontes No more such wives; therefore, no wife: one worse,
And better used, would make her sainted spirit
Again possess her corpse, and on this stage
(Were we offenders now) appear soul-vex'd,
And begin, 'Why to me?' . . .

Paulina Were I the ghost that walk'd, I'd bid you mark
Her eye, and tell me for what dull part in't
You chose her: then I'd shriek, that even your ears
Should rift to hear me; and the words that follow'd
Should be 'Remember mine'. . . .
Yet, if my lord will marry, . . .
                give me the office
To choose you a queen: she shall not be so young
As was your former, but she shall be such
As walk'd your first queen's ghost, it should take joy
To see her in your arms. (76)

In preparing for her return to the play, therefore, Shakespeare seeks, without spoiling the surprise that is to come, to arouse in the audience a condition of some suspense in relation to Hermione, and of some degree of preparedness for marvel.

III

The remainder of the scene is devoted to the young. But Shake-speare knows where he wants the emphasis to lie and it is not primarily on them. It is on Leontes. The young are a vital part of the play but not the main part.

There are three further sections: the announcement of the young people's arrival (85–122); their entrance and welcome (123–77); the news that Polixenes also has arrived, in hot pursuit (177–232).

The first of these is conducted conspicuously in terms of the praise of Perdita. To give time for this, due ceremony is observed, and lords are sent to greet the royal couple. The praise of Perdita and the accompanying delay arouse expectancy, of course, which must be satisfied (as far as possible) by the delight of her appear-ance when she does enter. This emphasis gives her special atten-tion without involving her in the ensuing dialogue. From the point of view of the plot it is both safe and proper that she should keep quiet and let Florizel do the talking. For the dramatist's purposes it is important that the praise of Perdita's good looks should not be voiced—or at least not voiced first and most loudly—by Leontes. So Shakespeare makes the servant who announces the young couple's approach no ordinary servant but also a court poet. The poet cannot mention Perdita without running to superlatives (87, 94); but there is no touch of satire of courtly extravagance in the writing of the part. He speaks with the enthusiasm yet essential truth of a votary. When Paulina inter-venes on behalf of Hermione, formerly the chief object of his praise, he avoids making comparison but stands his ground: when she sees Perdita, he says, even Paulina will approve of her! (105)

Before the happy meeting—the second section distinguished above—there is a sudden contrasting note of pain and apprehen-sion. Paulina recalls Mamillius, equating him with the Florizel they are about to see:

> Had our prince
> (Jewel of children) seen this hour, he had pair'd
> Well with this lord: there was not a full month
> Between their births. (115)

Only at this point does Leontes show signs of breaking under the strain of Paulina's relentless campaign of recollection and reproof:

> Prithee, no more; cease; thou know'st
> He dies to me again, when talk'd of: sure,
> When I shall see this gentleman, thy speeches
> Will bring me to consider that which may
> Unfurnish me of reason.

Such are the depths of his unspoken sense of loss. That way madness quite possibly could lie, even still.[1]

Thus Shakespeare at the last moment gives Leontes' meeting with Florizel and Perdita the additional character, in expectation, of a confrontation with his past. It is for Leontes to sustain this section: all that Florizel has to do is to play the part prepared for him by Camillo (IV, iv, 557). It is an excellent idea, therefore, in throwing the weight of the encounter upon Leontes to extend its levels of interest. Leontes fears what may happen when he sees in Florizel the young man Mamillius might have become; but that is not the way things work out. Prepared to meet his past he sees in Florizel not Mamillius but Polixenes, the occasion indeed of self-reproach (133, 146, 170), but also of happy memory and hope for the future (127, 136); for in recalling the time when he and Polixenes were twenty-one (125) his thoughts run back to long before his fall at the beginning of the play. And the arresting sight of Perdita in Florizel's company, as he turns to greet her also, makes him think not of Mamillius only but of both his lost children. So he thinks of him not merely with self-reproach but in the light of his admiration for this angelic pair:

> Most dearly welcome!
> And your fair princess,—goddess!—O, alas!
> I lost a couple, that 'twixt heaven and earth
> Might thus have stood, begetting wonder, as
> You, gracious couple, do.   (129)

Similarly inclusive benevolence and free use of the thought and language of piety is found also in Leontes' last speech in this section:

[1] This delicate touch would appear to derive from the clumsy conclusion of *Pandosto* (which Greene calls closing up the comedy with a tragical stratagem), where after the wedding of the two young lovers the king meditates on his former crimes and, falling into a melancholy fit, kills himself (p. 225).

> The blessed gods
> Purge all infection from our air whilst you
> Do climate here! You have a holy father,
> A graceful gentleman: against whose person
> (So sacred as it is) I have done sin,
> For which, the heavens (taking angry note)
> Have left me issueless: and your father's blest
> (As he from heaven merits it) with you,
> Worthy his goodness. What might I have been,
> Might I a son and daughter now have look'd on,
> Such goodly things as you![1] (167)

A moment before, Leontes wondered at Polixenes for having exposed 'this paragon' (Perdita) to the perils of the sea (152), ironically reminding us of his own ill usage of her as an infant. Now the irony of the situation is reversed. Here is evidence that the gods' anger is assuaged, for the issue of the 'issueless' king now stands before him. He, no less than Polixenes, is 'blest', for one of the 'goodly things' he looks on is his own daughter: he has a share in the brave new world of youth (177).

It gives an audience a sense of well-being to know something about a character on the stage of which he himself is ignorant. Hence that Leontes is unaware of his blessing enhances the effect of the situation; and it may therefore be regarded as a well-calculated substitute for a 'recognition' scene upon the stage. Leontes' warm feeling goes out spontaneously to these admirable young people. It is a tribute partly to their youth and beauty, partly to his friend Polixenes in his son. It is, that is to say, entirely benevolent. Awareness that his long-lost daughter has been restored, that the oracle has been fulfilled, would introduce selfish motives: the motive of satisfaction that he has an heir, the motive of satisfaction that the wrong he has done to himself and her has been undone. In a word, to follow this meeting of Leontes and Perdita with a 'recognition' scene would be redundant. On

[1] It would be out of place to cavil at 'a holy father' as an accurate description of Polixenes after the mood we saw him in in the last scene. Leontes is speaking once more as the flower of courtesy, now spiritually restored if still somewhat storm-tossed, and as benevolent age playing admiring host to youth and through it to restored friendship. This is a play which operates through mood and attitude more than character. In the last scene Polixenes was a device rather than a character. It is the beautiful young king of the first act that Leontes is thinking of now, the man whose image is called up by his beautiful young son.

the entrance of the lord, therefore, with the news of Polixenes'
arrival, Shakespeare lets us know that the secret is as good as out:
Polixenes and Camillo are in talk with the Old Shepherd, and a
'recognition' scene is perhaps hardly to be expected.

IV

The final section rounds off the scene both (1) as it concerns the
young people and (2) as it concerns Leontes. The crucial passage
comes towards the end:

Florizel   Beseech you, sir,
    Remember since you ow'd no more to time
    Than I do now: with thought of such affections,
    Step forth my advocate: at your request,
    My father will grant precious things as trifles.
Leontes Would he do so, I'd beg your precious mistress,
    Which he counts but a trifle.
Paulina   Sir, my liege,
    Your eye hath too much youth in't; not a month
    'Fore your queen died, she was more worth such gazes
    Than what you look on now.
Leontes   I thought of her,
    Even in these looks I made. But your petition
    Is yet unanswer'd. I will to your father:
    Your honour not o'erthrown by your desires,
    I am a friend to them and you.   (217)

(1) On Florizel's arrival Leontes greeted him thus:

                Were I but twenty-one,
    Your father's image is so hit in you,
    His very air, that I should call you brother
    As I did him, and speak of something wildly
    By us perform'd before.   (124)

Florizel now remembers those words and makes them the basis of
his appeal for support. Leontes has been concerned at hearing of
Florizel's breach of filial duty (210), but none the less takes on the
part of Camillo, one might say, as the help and defender of youth,
and agrees to speak on Florizel's behalf. His sympathy for the
young being grounded on the recollection of his own youth and

Polixenes', the continuity not opposition of youth and age is proclaimed.

(2) At the beginning of the scene there were indications that having purged his shame Leontes might be ready for married life again. The passage we are considering, in which Paulina reproves him for gazing at Perdita, seems to return to this matter. Does Leontes' impulse correspond in miniature to Pandosto's incestuous passion? J. H. P. Pafford appears to think so, writing, 'Worst of all is his desire for Perdita' (p. lxxiii).

That interpretation surely is impossible to justify. Leontes sees that Perdita is an attractive girl, as Polixenes and Camillo have done (IV, iv, 78, 85, 110, 156, 159, 174, 178, 368, 423, 426, 435, 442): that recognition is one of the points of the passage. But his attitude towards her has bordered on veneration. 'Goddess', 'paragon', and 'precious' (130, 152, 222) are not words suggestive of intended seduction. 'Precious', indeed, is Polixenes' epithet for Hermione herself (I, ii, 79, 452; IV, ii, 24). To Leontes, Florizel and Perdita seem angels begetting wonder, as his own children might have been had they lived (131), 'goodly things', eminently desirable as a son and daughter (176).

For Leontes to manifest 'desire' for Perdita would therefore be most inconsistent with his attitude towards her up to this point. Nor does the passage bear that interpretation. Even the vigilant and censorious Paulina cannot represent Leontes' gazes of admiration as lustful. She is still standing up for Hermione against Perdita in spite of the court poet's hopes. Hermione, she says, was worthier of Leontes' admiration than Perdita is (225). Leontes' little joke about begging to have Florizel's precious sweetheart for himself is quite consistent with his earlier wish that he could have her as a daughter.

'I thought of her [Hermione], / Even in these looks I made'. Does Shakespeare intend us to believe this, or to regard it as a lie to cover up guilty desire?[1] Leontes thought of Polixenes immediately he met Florizel; but then he was looking at him closely (126). He has had no occasion to scan Perdita's face—only to take general note of her being extraordinarily beautiful. He has had no occasion to do this—until Florizel says in effect, 'Think of yourself when you were a young man in love ("with thoughts of such

---

[1] That there is a resemblance between mother and daughter is made clear later. It is included in the recital of proofs of Perdita's identity (V, ii, 36).

affections"), and intercede for me'. Then, with his sweetheart Hermione in mind, he does look closely at the girl he has been asked to champion. And, there she is: the resemblance is plain— Hermione! No wonder he gazes. Shakespeare has made his point: Leontes is by no means averse from marriage, but Hermione is the wife he wants.

This final section is arranged like a sandwich, with Leontes' gazes in the middle, and Florizel's appeal and Leontes' answer on either side. In the middle we have Leontes' honourable love for his sweetheart Hermione revived and strengthened by a glimpse of Hermione in the young girl. Consequent upon the heartening recollection is his willingness to support the young man and his desires, provided that they too are honourable:

> Your honour not o'erthrown by your desires,
> I am friend to them and you.

The man who has sinned against honour is now its champion. Leontes' answer may be conditional in form, but in acting on it at once without further inquiry he ranges himself with Perdita in her ardent romanticism:

> By th' pattern of mine own thoughts I cut out
> The purity of his.   (IV, iv, 383)

Shakespeare has forgiven Leontes.[1]

Scene Two

I

So Shakespeare substitutes for a 'recognition' scene on the stage a meeting between Leontes and Perdita in which by spontaneous admiration and championship in adversity the king unwittingly

---

[1] John Lawlor has a valuable passage (pp. 102–3) on this scene. I may in general confirmation of my own conclusions quote two of the points he makes. Of ll. 151f. ('Welcome hither / As is the spring to th'earth'): 'the hospitality we had seen violently strained in Act I, Scene ii is now fulfilled'. Of Leontes' admiration of Perdita: 'It is Shakespeare's transmutation of Greene's incest-theme; and it is at once related to Leontes' sense of unalterable loss. . . . Time past is bridged; a youthful Hermione is ever-present to Leontes' mind'.

does what is possible to compensate for the wrongs that must stand between them. No doubt the emotional difficulties involved could have been glossed over in a scene of direct confrontation of shamefaced father and new-found daughter, without thus first establishing a sympathetic relationship; but glossing over is not enough. Besides, somewhat similar difficulties will arise in the final scene. It is wise, therefore, to avoid the challenge in this place, show father and daughter meeting on warm and friendly terms, and then leave the recognition to be reported.

Reported by whom, and to whom? At the time of the discovery everyone of consequence will be in the royal presence. The choice lies, then, between discussion after the event (say, between Polixenes and Camillo) and news brought hotfoot by lesser courtiers to lesser courtiers. The second alternative has the great advantage of giving immediacy of effect, the excitement of the moment; but it lacks the merit of the first, that of involving speakers already known to us. Can this defect be supplied? Who is available to supply it? Cleomenes and Dion would be of the royal entourage. The only other character left who is known to us and uninvolved is Autolycus. He has assurance enough for anything, and experience of a sort in playing the gentleman. He would serve to maintain continuity; but what is there for him to do? To provide comedy, obviously. Where lesser courtiers are concerned there can certainly be an element of comedy, giving variety to the recital of the news, but this must not be of a kind that will distract the mind from the recital. The performance of Autolycus's normal comic functions will have to wait, therefore, to the end of the scene, where we can take final leave of him and his partners in comedy, the Old Shepherd and the Clown. The scene does not take place 'Before Leontes' palace', as the editors unaccountably have it, but in one of the waiting-rooms where gentlemen in waiting chat and gossip endlessly, constantly on the look out for news to relieve the tedium. There in the pride of their new-won gentility the Old Shepherd and his son may later be met with propriety, after displaying the evidences of Perdita's birth, instead of being hustled down the back stairs like rustics.

The account of the recognition is, then, to be in the hands of minor courtiers, with Autolycus to act as a thread of continuity both with the past (suggesting comic treatment), and with the concluding passage of the scene. Continuity has also been provided

by the brief anticipatory mention in the previous scene of the
impending discovery, in terms which also suggest comic treatment.
Polixenes and Camillo have met the clowns, and Camillo has them
in question:

> Never saw I
> Wretches so quake: they kneel, they kiss the earth;
> Forswear themselves as often as they speak.
> Bohemia stops his ears, and threatens them
> With divers deaths in death.   (V, i, 197)

The passage is neatly sewn into place by making the news provoke
Perdita's only speech of the scene:

> O my poor father!
> The heaven sets spies upon us, will not have
> Our contract celebrated.

Her daughterly feeling has betrayed her into letting the cat out of
the bag: she is not married nor (so she thinks) is she the daughter
of a king. Leontes rises to the occasion, and her daughterly feeling
may the more easily transfer itself to him.

II

In this play at any rate Shakespeare does everything at the top of
his bent. 'Leaving to be reported' does no mean fobbing off with
the second best. If he avoids the challenge of a recognition scene
upon the stage it is to accept another and more novel challenge, at
least as interesting from the technical point of view. How can an
exchange of news between lesser courtiers be made worthy to
stand in the penultimate position in the play? Does such an exchange not rather suggest one of those passages of introduction
set at the beginning of the first four acts? Like the opening scene
of the play this one does not involve leading characters directly
but looks at them from the outside, and it will fittingly be conducted in prose. Are there possible advantages here to explore?
Prose, certainly, need not be prosaic; and as Delius observed of
the completed scene, 'We have an amusing offset to the cere-
monious and artistic prose of the earlier portion of the scene in the
downright prose of the two Clowns with their delicious simplicity

over their newly born nobility'. The combination of ceremony and
dilettantism in courtly fashion can be used to lighten the manner
of the gentlemen's recital. The news they bring is full of delightful
surprise and mounting excitement. Wonder and excitement are
infectious; so are their display upon the stage. Excitement runs to
hyperbole; yet some quality of detachment may also be expected
in fine gentlemen mightily interested and concerned but not also
actively involved: and this combination too may occasion a lighter
touch.

The special flavour of the scene, however, arises out of the
nature of the lesser courtier's profession: he is a looker-on, a
spectator of life, a spectator at the play of life. The events described are narrated as a kind of dumb-show. After the fardel was
opened, we learn, the first gentleman and his like were dismissed
from the presence chamber. He had already heard something of
what the Old Shepherd had to tell, and as he went out thought he
heard more, but these are all things we know already. What
concerns us to know is what he saw when he was out of earshot,
the wordless exchange of looks between Leontes and Camillo:

> there was speech in their dumbness, language in their very gesture;
> they looked as they had heard of a world ransomed, or one destroyed:
> a notable passion of wonder appeared in them; but the wisest be-
> holder, that knew no more but seeing, could not say if th' impor-
> tance were joy or sorrow; but in the extremity of the one it must
> needs be. (13)

The effect, that of a transfixed state of becoming, of a fulness of
significance held just short of bursting point, is remarkably
appropriate, and is due to the deliberate economy of means,
knowing 'no more but seeing'. The question is held static: a
world ransomed or one destroyed?—extreme joy or extreme
sorrow? We, the spectators, know the answer; but for the play-
world this is the supreme moment of suspense, and the novel
method of proclaiming it enables us to share the suspense.

The answer comes at once and abruptly, with the hurried
entrance of another gentleman. 'The news?' Public rejoicing,
bonfires, ballads. The oracle is fulfilled; the king's daughter is
found. It is a world ransomed, not a world destroyed. The price
has been paid: Leontes' world has been freed from its past
captivity.

A third man bustles in, confirming the wonderful news, so that we now have four excited men on the stage. This is Paulina's steward, a man of some authority not commanded out of the presence chamber, and so able to report all the details. He mentions the proofs and then continues:

Gentleman 3. Did you see the meeting of the two kings?
Gentleman 2. No.
Gentleman 3. Then have you lost a sight which was to be seen, cannot be spoken of. . . . There was casting up of eyes, holding up of hands, with countenance of such distraction, that they were to be known by garment, not by favour. Our king, being ready to leap out of himself for joy of his found daughter, as if that joy were now become a loss, cries 'O, thy mother, thy mother!':[1] then asks Bohemia forgiveness; then embraces his son-in-law: then again worries he his daughter with clipping her; now he thanks the old shepherd, which stands by, like a weather-bitten conduit of many kings' reigns. I never heard of such another encounter, which lames report to follow it, and undoes description to do it.   (40)

It will be noted that this gentleman too deals mainly in looks and gestures rather than words, and that this helps the dramatist, avoiding dramatic representation of the events described, to give them a forced, serio-comic air. Courtly prose proves to be an admirable means of doing this; and the melodramatic, play-within-the-play effect is raised still further by our being invited to exaggerate it in our minds, the sight being beyond verbal description, we are told, and needing to be seen to yield its full effect.[2]

---

[1] Shakespeare has his eye here on Greene's description of Pandosto's meeting with his daughter:

> he suddenly leapt from his seat and kissed Fawnia, wetting her tender cheeks with his tears, and crying, 'My daughter Fawnia! ah sweet Fawnia! I am thy father, Fawnia'. (p. 224)

'Suddenly leapt from his seat' is replaced by the more exciting 'leap out of himself for joy'; but Leontes' readiness to do this is held back by his much more powerful sense of loss, and his cry becomes not 'My daughter Perdita' but 'O, thy mother, thy mother!' The recognition scene thus becomes an incidental pointer to Leontes' need of Hermione's return.

[2] Furness (*New Variorum Shakespeare, The Winter's Tale* (1898) p. 279) makes the odd mistake of supposing that if Shakespeare had not used the method of report through dramatic dialogue he would have staged the events described, and staged them as they are described. He believes that Shakespeare

Perdita's discovery is the occasion of all the joy and tears, but she is far from being the centre of the narrator's attention. He is a Sicilian courtier. He calls the incident 'the meeting of the two kings': it is his own king that he is interested in. He is also the Lady Paulina's steward, and when the talk turns to the fate of Antigonus she is the second topic on which he dilates. He paints two contrasting pictures. The first was one of general emotional confusion, joy wading in tears, features blurred, the central figure impulsively starting out in joy and sorrow towards all four surrounding figures at once, only one of whom—a tearful old gargoyle—is sketched in any detail. The subject of the second picture also is joy and sorrow, but now there is no feeling of crowding, movement, excitement. There are two figures only, and the impression conveyed is that of stillness and strong composure, the devotion of the kneeling girl, the deep thankfulness of her champion in infancy. Paulina

> had one eye declined for the loss of her husband, another elevated that the oracle was fulfilled: she lifted the princess from the earth, and so locks her in embracing as if she would pin her to her heart, that she might no more be in danger of losing. (74)

Shakespeare shows great tact in thus reserving Paulina and Perdita for separate notice, treating them as detached from the mêlée, and thus quietly emphasizing the private as distinct from the public aspect of the situation and paying silent tribute to Paulina for her part in the affair. He also uses the occasion to bring Paulina to prominence, now that the statue and the final scene are in prospect.

In that passage Paulina's steward seems perhaps rather more involved in his subject than elsewhere. His normal standpoint, like his friends', is that of the connoisseur of courtly feeling, attitude and effect. Their interest is centred equally upon matter and manner. They speak as spectators rather than participants.

---

was 'afraid of his actors', afraid that they might turn 'deep and tragic emotion' into 'not merely comedy, but even farce':

> merely let us vividly picture to ourselves what might be fairly termed the joyous, ebullient antics of Leontes, first begging pardon of Polixenes, then hugging Florizel, then worrying Perdita with his embraces, then wringing the old shepherd's hand, who was crying vigorously and probably with superfluous noise,—and I think we shall be quite aware that unless all the characters were assumed by actors of commanding power, the scene would degenerate into farce and end amid uproarious jeers.

Continuing now to savour the delightful artifice of the scene (as with their courtly training they regard it), the gentlemen, amateurs of the fine art of life, proceed with their critical appreciation:

Gentleman 1. The dignity of this act was worth the audience of kings and princes; for by such was it acted.

Gentleman 3. One of the prettiest touches of all, and that which angled for mine eyes (caught the water though not the fish) was, when at the relation of the queen's death (with the manner how she came to 't bravely confessed and lamented by the king) how attentiveness wounded his daughter. (79)

It is a transitional passage, leading in thought through Hermione's death and Perdita's grief at hearing of it to Hermione's statue and Perdita's desire to see it. The parenthetical mention of Leontes' brave confession and lamentation is not, perhaps, essential in the context, but it comes very well here and in this manner, insulated by reported speech against causing embarrassment in the audience. Immediately she becomes known to him Leontes is free and open with his daughter on this most painful subject, and at this point when Hermione is finally returning to view his continued lamentation for his behaviour towards her is fittingly glanced at.

The notes of 'wonder' (16, 23), 'a world ransomed' (15), and likeness to an old tale (28, 62) have been preparing us for the final scene. Antigonus is dead; yet the infant lives, the oracle is fulfilled: news 'so like an old tale that the verity of it is in strong suspicion' is nevertheless true. We have been put in a mood to believe marvels. The statue, now brought to knowledge for the first time, is spoken of as a marvel: the sculptor, Giulio Romano,

> had he himself eternity and could put creation into his work, would beguile Nature of her custom, so perfectly he is her ape: he so near to Hermione hath done Hermione, that they say one would speak to her and stand in hope of answer. (96)

No one can say that if the statue moves we have not been warned. Likewise if we wish to reconcile its moving with common sense we have the second gentleman's statement that ever since the death of Hermione, Paulina has privately twice or thrice a day visited the removed house where she keeps the statue (104).[1]

---

[1] The steward has explained that the piece was 'many years in doing, and now newly perform'd [i.e."lately finished", *or* "freshly recoloured, with added wrinkles"], by that rare Italian master, Julio Romano'.

Whetting our appetite with their eagerness for good things to come, they go to see it:

> Every wink of an eye, some new grace will be born: our absence makes us unthrifty to our knowledge. Let's along.[1]   (110)

III

As they go, Autolycus takes the opportunity of picking a pocket to show that he has the dash of his former life in him (113); and so, wisely, he remains behind. Starting the scene in the company of a gentleman, he aroused momentary expectancy of a scene of broad comedy in which he would take a leading part; but soon he was pushed aside in the excitement. Now he is left to break his unaccustomed silence with accustomed informatory monologue. With pleasant pedantry he answers a question that had occurred to Shakespeare in reading Greene's tale: how was it that when the Old Shepherd had the evidence of Perdita's birth on board ship Florizel did not think to look at it then, so that it remained to be disclosed on shore? The answer is that he and Perdita were too seasick to think about anything else. Romance lays itself open to many a pin-prick.

Shakespeare read with evident delight in Greene that 'Pandosto, willing to recompense old Porrus, of a shepherd made him a knight'. This, he must have felt, was too good to lose. It was just the sort of probable improbability to base a scene of low comedy on; but not 'a knight': *gentlemen*,—father and son—to round off a scene of fine gentlemen. It is, when one comes to think of it, but plain justice to make Perdita's life-long father and brother gentlemen now that she is a princess, for where would she have been without them?

The topsy-turvydom admirably inverts the tone and so sets off the courtly dignity of the next scene. The three fine gentlemen

[1] We may recall Dion's similar little advertisement as he and Cleomenes return with the oracle:
> something rare
> Even then will rush to knowledge. Go: fresh horses!
> And gracious be the issue.   (III, i, 20)

If we do, there is counter-irony in the later scene in that the speaker's expectation is realized not dashed, and that the issue here is indeed gracious.

give place to the swaggering, clownish gentleman who picks a quarrel and swears to the truth of falsehood like a gentleman born any time these four hours. He and his father, the tables being turned, are now graciously pleased to grant the mock-obsequious request of one whom not long before they bribed as 'a great courtier'. In their gentility father and son suggest a satirical contrast: for the Old Shepherd rank means obligation ('we must be gentle, now we are gentlemen'); for the Clown it means privilege ('Let boors and franklins say it, I'll swear it'). But 'twere to consider too curiously to consider so: the comedy is unmixed: the Clown may have the makings of a braggart and a bully in him, but at present he is just enjoying himself hugely, nothing more. We remember best his unconscious parody of the meeting of the two kings:

> I was a gentleman born before my father; for the king's son took me by the hand, and called me brother; and then the two kings called my father brother; and then the prince, my brother, and the princess, my sister, called my father father; and so we wept; and there was the first gentleman-like tears that ever we shed. (139)

This section of the scene undoubtedly belongs to the Clown. In neither section does Autolycus appear to advantage. In the first he is a hanger-on, marking time, awaiting his chance; in the second he is getting a taste of his own medicine. Lorded over by the gentleman clowns he is in a similar situation to theirs at the end of the previous act when they were lorded over by him, a 'gentleman' pedlar. The possibility of his reinstatement in the service of the prince, his 'master' as he likes to call him (151), is raised presumably by way of compensation; and, though the question is left in the air he is assured in the very last word of the scene that he will no longer be legally a 'masterless' man, whatever happens. In the circumstances he is unwontedly subdued and is given few opportunities to show his resourcefulness and subacid wit (136, 155 [cf. IV, iv, 716], 169); but he is still 'a tall fellow of his hands',[1] and 'proves so' in the last glimpse we have of him (169), when with grave humility he picks his benefactor's pocket, as he did when we met him first (IV, iii, 75). So doing, he obediently follows his 'good masters' as they go out through one door to

[1] In the old sense ('skilful with his hands', here 'nimble fingered'), not in the fashionable sense which the Clown is parading ('formidable with weapons'). *O.E.D.*, *s.v.* tall 4; Pafford, p. 153.

enter no doubt with the train at another, thus helping to fill the stage for the final scene. The kings and the princes are going to see the statue, and the clowns must join their 'kindred'.

Scene Three

I

The play draws to a close. Full payment has, it seems, been made. Leontes has redeemed all faults, 'indeed paid down / More penitence than done trespass' (v, i, 3); a world has been ransomed; Paulina feels fully recompensed: her services are at an end:

Leontes O grave and good Paulina, the great comfort
            That I have had of thee!
Paulina   What, sovereign sir,
            I did not well, I meant well. All my services
            You have paid home.

What she has yet to do she will perform not as one of the duties of her self-appointed office, but as honoured hostess to the royal family: the king, his heir and daughter, her contracted husband, and his father, the boyhood friend and 'brother' of the king.

The royal group, last seen together in the first act, is reunited, a family party.[1] Florizel takes the place of Mamillius, who is now not mentioned; and as for Hermione, she is to be replaced by another, of Paulina's choosing, 'As like Hermione as is her picture', but only when the 'queen's again in breath'. Meanwhile her statue stands, in the chapel of Paulina's removed house, the work of a sculptor who, though he cannot 'put breath into his work', has made her speaking likeness. Everyone has come to see it, confident of some exciting experience to come, and impatient to swell the rejoicing that the oracle has been fulfilled.

[1] In the last scene their meeting was reported. In the shorthand of the drama, that marked the end of the estrangement. There is now no danger of awkwardness or embarrassment. They are close friends.

II

The concentration is intense. There is a full stage from the start. All eyes are fixed one way. There are no distractions, no rival interests, no comings and goings, at times hardly a movement or a breath: 'all stand still. . . . No foot shall stir' (95).[1] There are only two principal speakers, and even as we listen to them we watch the statue, for it is of the statue that they talk. One person conducts the proceedings, stirring, controlling, and guiding Leontes' responses. In him Paulina has a highly impressionable subject, and as his excitement mounts so does everyone else's, both on the stage and in the audience.

There is talk on the stage, but there is also silence. When the statue is discovered all stand silent in wonder (21): Leontes has to be called upon to speak. Perdita stands 'like stone' (42) before her stone mother. Hermione's descent naturally strikes 'all that look upon with marvel' (100); and Paulina has to urge Leontes not to shun his wife and to present his hand. As he holds back, Hermione, in token of forgiveness, embraces him and hangs about his neck, but with no sobs of joy or happy cries—silently, as befits this noble lady, dignified and composed, returned as from the dead. They exchange no word, but share 'a little while' of silence (118). Hermione's attention has to be drawn to Perdita as the girl kneels silent before her, so wholehearted has been her spontaneous welcome for Leontes. Then she speaks, calling down the graces of the gods on her daughter's head, kissing her no doubt as she raises her up and asks lovingly about her. But that way chat and reminiscence lie, and these are firmly to be kept till afterwards (152). Paulina is at hand to forbid any such tendency for the present (128). Restraint is the keynote. Hermione is given one speech only. Perdita does not speak after the statue comes to life. Florizel does not speak at any time.

[1] Shakespeare is very confident of holding his audience when he can write these lines:
Paulina   Shall I draw the curtain?
Leontes No: not these twenty years.
Perdita   *So long could I*
        Stand by, a looker on.

III

The sight of the statue revives Leontes' remorse and shame (24, 34, 40, 37)—mingled with and sharpened by his grateful memory of Hermione's worth (32, 25).[1] He now has friends to relieve and support him (49, 53), but yet he is highly wrought (58). To his hypersensitive mind the statue seems to combine with the attributes of majesty a quality of magic, conjuring his evils to remembrance and turning his living daughter to stone. Perdita, caught up in the emotion, is moved to kneel to the statue, not superstitiously as to a mere statuary saint but deliberately as though it were indeed her mother (39, 45). Womanly common sense is her characteristic contribution to the atmosphere of veneration and supernatural wonder. Under Paulina's guidance, sight stimulates Leontes' fancy to such an extent that he is prepared to forsake the world of sense and spend the rest of his life imagining that Hermione really is alive (71, 84).[2] From that it is but a step for the

---

[1] These passages are most effective in sending the mind back over the play, helping to knit it up. The delight and admiration with which Leontes recalls Hermione's dignified unhurried ardour during their courtship—

> O, thus she stood,
> Even with such life of majesty, warm life,
> As now it coldly stands, when first I woo'd her!—   (34)

tellingly contrast with the cynical destructiveness of his recollections when jealousy began to take hold on him:

> Why, that was when
> Three crabbed months had sour'd themselves to death
> Ere I could make thee open thy white hand,
> And clap thyself my love.

And Leontes' first words to the statue when it is discovered likewise give the measure of his regeneration:

> . . . or rather, thou art she
> In thy not chiding; for she was as tender
> As infancy and grace.   (25)

The tenderness of infancy and grace meant nothing to him when in his hardness of heart he sinned so cruelly against his daughter and his wife.

[2] As John Lawlor puts it (p. 103), 'the statue awakens an impossible longing; and the illusion that it lives is preferable to reality'. Quoting the next two lines—

> No settled senses of the world can match
> The pleasure of that madness—

object of his imagination to be realized, under the exercise of faith not wicked powers (95, 91).

This is to say, there is a Pygmalionic element in the affair, anticipated by Paulina's words in the central scene when she announced Hermione's death:

> If you can bring
> Tincture, or lustre in her lip, her eye,
> Heat outwardly or breath within, I'll serve you
> As I would do the gods.   (III, ii, 204)

Here Leontes seems to help to bring the statue to life, in gazing on it:

Paulina   No longer shall you gaze on't, lest your fancy
            May think anon it moves.
Leontes   Let be, let be!
            Would I were dead, but that methinks already—
            What was he that did make it?—See, my lord,
            Would you not deem it breath'd? and that those veins
            Did verily bear blood?
Polixenes   Masterly done:
            The very life seems warm upon her lip.
Leontes   The fixure of her eye has motion in't,
            As we are mock'd with art.   (60)

In the reanimation of Hermione, then, the ardent anticipation of Leontes seems a contributory condition. But in the case of

---

he calls Leontes' illusion 'the joyous counterpart of Pandosto's "desperate thoughts"'.

I prefer to see those lines as a correlative of Florizel's affirmation,

> If my reason
> Will thereto be obedient, I have reason;
> If not, my senses, better pleas'd with madness
> Do bid it [my fancy = my love] welcome.   (IV, iv, 483)

In both cases these are dangerously insecure foundations to build upon, but in this world of romance, both men, being pure and true in their anti-rational faith, are rewarded with wonderful good fortune. Leontes' willing surrender to illusion here—delighted, rapt in admiration, selfless—contrasts in every particular with his willing surrender to illusion in the first act, and may perhaps be taken as a symbolical act of atonement.

As for Pandosto's 'desperate thoughts'—leading him to suicide in a fit of melancholy—a counterpart to these is, as I have suggested (*ante*, p. 105), to be seen in V, i, where Leontes fears that at the sight of Florizel, reminding him of Mamillius, he will be brought 'to consider that which may / Unfurnish [him] of reason'.

Pygmalion divine intervention was necessary to breathe life into the image; and Paulina is no Venus, nor yet a Medea—'assisted by wicked powers' (90)—to call up dead men from their graves. She is neither more nor less than Paulina. She claims that she can make the statue move indeed, but does not claim that she can do it by magic; and she uses no hocus pocus:

> Music: awake her: strike:
> 'Tis time: descend: be stone no more: approach:
> Strike all that look upon with marvel: come:
> I'll fill your grave up: stir: nay, come away:
> Bequeath to death your numbness: for from him
> Dear life redeems you—you perceive she stirs.   (98)

The only aid Paulina requires is that Leontes should 'awake' his faith (94). She applies the initial stimulus by calling for music; she announces that ''Tis time', and that 'dear life' redeems Hermione, but she does not speak as their agent or the manipulator of their operations. It is the music, not she, that awakens the sleeper;[1] time has been fulfilled, and therefore Hermione can descend; it is 'dear life' that redeems from death. Paulina encourages and directs, like one assisting at a birth, but the recreative processes are not of her ordering.

The heavy pointing of the passage, remarked on by Nevill Coghill, is suggestive of the difficulties involved. Hermione must wake, cease to be stone, move, walk. This requires repeated, muscular commands. We must understand that for stone to become flesh, for rigidity to become mobile, calls for much effort and encouragement. That this is no wicked spirit disguised as Hermione, but Hermione herself returned in this theatrical fashion from death is indicated by the reference to her grave.[2] Paulina can promise to fill that up; but it took 'dear life' to free Hermione from it, to perform this crowning act of redemption in the play, turning the numbness of stone to warm life.

This is a transformation scene. The effect aimed at is that of a statue coming to life, not of a woman pretending to be a statue and

---

[1] For the power of music as an accompaniment to restoration, cf. *K.L.* IV, vii, 25 and *Per.* III, ii, 90.

[2] 'I'll fill your grave up'. It seems not unlikely that the words have been preserved from a stage in the writing in which Hermione stood as a statue on her own tomb.

then pretending gradually to come to life. It is essentially theatrical. It would be out of its element in the world of narrative:

> That she is living
> *Were it but told you*, should be hooted at
> Like an old tale; (115)

and that would never do. The least suspicion of a smile would ruin the effect. The events related in V, ii were, considered in the total context of the play, all the more effective for being reported as contrived, posed, arranged, *as though* performed upon a stage. This event, on the other hand, *is* and must be performed upon the stage. It must be seen to be believed. Its impact must be direct. Paulina's commands produce tension, physical excitement. The words,

> Start not: her actions shall be holy, as
> You hear my spell is lawful,

are addressed as much to the audience as to the persons on the stage. Even Leontes, who wanted to kiss his wife when it only seemed (77) that she breathed, now has to be restrained from shunning her when he sees her stir, so powerful is the impression of metamorphosis. Likewise with the audience. For the moment we go beyond the normal condition of dramatic illusion, in which what passes on the stage is accepted as a semblance of reality as seen in a special kind of mirror customarily used for the purpose. Here the experience is much more akin to delusion: briefly, but almost completely, we allow ourselves to be *possessed* by the magic of the theatre.

IV

The mood of the transformation scene must be held for a time, and allowed to dissolve only gradually. Leontes' fervour, Paulina's dignity, the *bona fides* of the whole affair, must be maintained and confirmed. To shatter the mood abruptly would ruin everything. The shock would savour of banana-skin comedy and would brand the reanimation as a hoax, a mere device for restoring Hermione, devoid of high seriousness. Hence Shakespeare is at pains not to treat the reunion of Leontes and Hermione in realistic terms. Intimate exchanges on the domestic level, in any case a source of embarrassment, would be quite out of keeping. In all the circumstances grief for a world destroyed, joy for a world ransomed—here as in V, ii—are best conveyed in dumb show. Everything points to the use of stylization—gesture and tableau, distanced by observers' commentary:

Polixenes   She embraces him!
Camillo   She hangs about his neck!

The moment of reunion is thus protracted and emphasized by making it the object of comment, inquiry and contemplation by those around. So long as Hermione remains silent the spell is unbroken; but the audience must soon begin asking questions and Shakespeare must be ready with his answers—must indeed start raising the questions first. Will he try to maintain the affair on the level of mystery; will he drop to the everyday factual level; or will he seek a conclusion capable of dual interpretation?

Broadly speaking, what he does is to attempt by easy stages to transfer the emphasis from the sense of wonder to rational explanation without abandoning the validity of the successive stages. With that end in view the device of making Hermione return *silent* is most effective. Until she speaks it is doubtful whether she is alive, and so the sense of mystery is prolonged. Until she speaks she cannot volunteer explanatory information, and so common sense remains in abeyance. Paulina, Shakespeare's special agent in the affair up to this point, does not talk of making Hermione speak: she is concerned with seeing not hearing, with actions not words (87, 104). On the other hand Leontes before the event, and Camillo after it, see that the transformation is incomplete if unaccompanied by the power of speech (91, 113). Special prominence, therefore, is given by anticipation to the moment when Hermione utters her maternal benediction; and protracting the tension beyond the breaking point (from stone to life) permits the shortening of the ensuing emotional relaxation which concludes the play.

When, reassured by Paulina, Leontes takes Hermione by the hand 'O she's warm', he exclaims:

> If this be magic, let it be an art
> Lawful as eating.   (109)

He has shunned her as perhaps something evil and forbidden, and now the touch of her is good, completely natural, so natural that it may be asked whether this is a case of magic at all. If it is magic, it must be lawful magic, 'natural magic', indeed the magic of nature itself. But Leontes is not rationalizing the affair, looking for an explanation. He is a man who has been deprived of his wife for sixteen years, and is concerned at the moment only with the magic of reunion. Camillo, lacking the evidence of touch, wonders whether Hermione is really alive, and wishes for the evidence of hearing: 'let her speak too'. 'Ay', says Polixenes: then she could 'make it manifest where she has liv'd, / Or how stolen from the dead'. These questions are raised now, when Hermione does not speak, so that with dramatic propriety they need not be raised when she does. Meanwhile, Paulina confines attention to Camillo's doubt, 'If she pertain to life' (113). That she is living, she says, is an idea stranger than the most improbable fiction; 'but it appears she lives, / Though yet she speak not'. For the dramatic purpose of preserving the sense of mystery this is a good answer. It puts first things first. Hermione is alive: that is what matters, not where she has been, whether on this side of the grave or on the other. It accords with what Paulina said earlier (V, i, 41) about how 'monstrous' it was to our human reason that the oracle should be fulfilled. It appears to put Hermione's restoration on the same footing as Perdita's: Perdita's seemed like an old tale, yet proved true: so this, which also seems like an old tale, may need no other proof than the evidence of our own eyes. And that Hermione cannot speak 'yet' suggests, of course, that mysterious forces are at work. At line 118 she still 'speak[s] not'. At line 119 Paulina, stage-managing almost to the last, asks Perdita to 'kneel / And pray [her] mother's blessing'. The explanation, we are apparently to understand, is that Hermione cannot speak until she knows that Perdita is found—that the presence of Perdita is necessary to complete her mother's restoration to full possession of her faculties.

For twenty lines, time on the stage has, so to speak, stood still. Paulina holds it back for 'a little while' longer so that all may mark the gracious couple, now no longer young, that stand 'twixt heaven and earth, begetting wonder. And then time on the stage seems to move again, and the glory and the dream fade slowly into something approaching the light of common day: the exaltation of high romance gives place to the delight of romantic comedy.

When Hermione stood as a statue Perdita knelt before it for blessing, uttering words which no live mother could listen to unmoved:

> Dear queen, that ended when I but began
> Give me that hand of yours to kiss.[1]   (42)

Now that Hermione is a live mother Paulina has to tell her that 'Our Perdita is found' (121). She is unaware that the oracle has been fulfilled and has to be informed of it. She was an inanimate statue, it appears, until she descended from her niche. Yet on the other hand Paulina's words, 'Our Perdita', indicate intimate joint concern, and suggest that she and Hermione had been awaiting this event over the years.[2]

V

That, then, is one solution—incompatible explanations left to be supposed somehow mysteriously compatible. Hermione's speech makes a fresh start:

---

[1] To amplify:

> Who euer is the mother of one chylde,
> Which hauing thought long dead, she fyndes aliue,
> Let her by proofe of that, which she hath fylde,
> In her owne breast, this mothers ioy descriue.
>
> (The Fairie Queene, VI, xii, 21)

But Hermoine the statue shows no such joy.

[2] 'Perdita is found' = that which was lost has been found. 'Our Perdita' = your Perdita and mine. The child's fate has been a special concern of Paulina's since its birth.

It was named to Antigonus in his dream by what he took to be the ghost of Hermione:

> and for the babe
> Is counted lost for ever, Perdita,
> I prithee, call't. (III, iii, 32)

Accordingly he left a note of the name with the child ('there lie, and there thy character'), so that she came to be known as Perdita in Bohemia. Paulina's expression, 'Our Perdita', savours of familiar use not lately acquired knowledge. If we look closely into the matter, therefore, it appears that Hermione gave the child its name in her own mind, communicating it (by thought transference!) to Antigonus in his dream, and telling it personally to Paulina.

126

> You gods, look down,
> And from your sacred vials pour your graces
> Upon my daughter's head! Tell me, mine own,
> Where hast thou been preserv'd? where liv'd? how found
> Thy father's court? for thou shalt hear that I,
> Knowing by Paulina that the oracle
> Gave hope thou wast in being, have preserv'd
> Myself to see the issue.   (121)

These words combine in one sweep of thought the gods (their blessing and their fiat in the oracle), Perdita (the object of both), and Hermione herself (who with motherly solicitude and pious confidence was, like her child, preserved, and has now, like her child, been found). Here the attitudes of rational explanation and of wonder may be seen not as incompatible but as mutually interpenetrating and supporting. They make a coherent whole.

Yet the *mere* common-sense level of explanation *is* strongly present. The preservation of Perdita and of Hermione are put on the same footing, but not now on the footing of 'old tale':

> Tell me, mine own,
> Where hast thou been preserv'd? where liv'd? how found
> Thy father's court?

We know the answers. The hushed and awe-struck girl need not reply.[1] Hermione's questions pass direct into her answer to the unspoken question how she has preserved herself. Thus simply, veils of mystery seem suddenly to be torn away. It is no longer a question if this be magic, if she pertain to life, or how she is stolen from the dead: Hermione has preserved herself (where is not now in question):

> for thou shalt hear that I,
> Knowing by Paulina that the oracle
> Gave hope thou wast in being, have preserv'd
> Myself to see the issue.

These words appear not to have been understood. It is customary to pass them over as evidence of Shakespeare's carelessness, since in fact Hermione herself heard the oracle read and did not

---

[1] Perdita's speech on her knees asking blessing has already been addressed to the statue. This enables Shakespeare, eschuing repetition, to make her the silent one now, and so, avoiding exchange of reminiscence, to preserve the tone of quiet dignity.

need to learn about it from Paulina.[1] Coleridge (I, 119) said categorically that Shakespeare did not provide in the oracle any 'ground for Hermione's seeming death and fifteen years . . . voluntary concealment'; and no one has contradicted him.

But here is first-hand evidence that the terms of the oracle did give Hermione hope and led her to preserve herself. It is true that she as well as Paulina was present when the oracle was read, but only Paulina saw its implication until she explained it to Hermione. As she said long afterwards, Paulina understood the pronouncement that

> the king shall live without an heir, *if that which is lost be not found*

to mean

> That King Leontes shall not have an heir
> *Till his lost child be found.* (V, i, 38)

That is to say, she saw in the condition 'if that which is lost be not found' a statement of the possibility of its own fulfilment.

The riddle of the oracle turns upon the ambiguity of the word lost, which means either (1) destroyed, dead or (2) mislaid, missing. In the first case what is lost has ceased to be; in the second there is at least hope that it exists and hence may be found. If the verb to find can be used in connexion with something lost, we know that that which is lost may exist. In the oracle this verb is used in connexion with the lost heir. That is why the oracle gave Paulina hope that Perdita was 'in being', and so why Hermione 'preserved herself' to see whether the hope was realized.[2]

So Hermione presents her preservation-and-restoration in two aspects, (a) emotional, mysterious, as due to the power of religious faith and motherly love, and (b) cerebral, matter-of-fact, as due to deliberate calculation. Its close association with the fulfilment of the oracle gives it the highest possible sanction, and at the same time (since oracles quibble) an element of rational comedy. To develop this comedy strain Shakespeare now takes up and extends the 'lost and found' motif (suggested by the oracle and appro-

[1] See, e.g., J. H. P. Pafford, pp. lii, 160.
[2] Antigonus, in contrast, understood the child to be destined for destruction, 'condemn'd' or 'expos'd' to 'loss' (II, iii, 191, III, iii, 50), and was himself 'lost too' (III, ii, 231), along with all the other 'instruments which aided to expose the child', who 'were even then lost when it was found' (V, ii, 70).

priate to the end of a romantic comedy), and, recalling that Leontes gave Paulina 'the office / To choose [him] a queen' (V, i, 77), unites the two ideas by a stroke of comedy-logic. Leontes has lost his wife; Paulina has found her. Paulina has lost her husband (he is 'never to be found again'; she will lament him till she is 'lost', i.e. dead, 134). So, says Leontes, he will find her another:

> Thou shouldst a husband take by my consent,
> As I by thine a wife: this is a match,
> And made between's by vows. Thou hast found mine;
> But how is to be question'd; for I saw her,
> As I thought, dead; and have in vain said many
> A prayer upon her grave. I'll not seek far—
> For him, I partly know his mind—to find thee
> An honourable husband. Come, Camillo,
> And take her by the hand.   (136)

Here is a piece of pure comedy routine. The old stagers are silently happy to be paired off by order and without warning. We more than partly know Camillo's mind—his acquisecene in any honourable bidding of his master's may be taken for granted—but when Paulina's is so pliant the spirit of fun is indeed in control and the stage of end-of-comedy convention has unmistakably been reached, when outstanding doubts or complications may be summarily resolved. Paulina's intended lamentations (132) are arbitrarily turned to joy; and all that remains is for the royal family (now completed by the restoration of the queen) happily to follow its hostess out of the chapel to exchange stories, as is often the way at the end of a comedy. Normal life is resumed as Leontes, for the first time since her return, speaks to his wife, begs her to exchange 'holy looks' once more with his 'brother', and introduces her to her son-in-law to be. The 'wide gap of time' is to be filled up (154). We are back where we started—except that it is sixteen years later. In the hasty conclusion proper to comedy, no account is taken of profit and loss.[1]

[1] Among the last plays, says Clifford Leech (*S.S.* 11, p. 30), 'only *The Winter's Tale* faces the realization that repentance is not enough, that "re-union" is a bogus word, that the only finality (within the world around us) is loss'. That suggests a bleak conclusion quite at variance with the sense of fullness and wonder pervading this scene, and it altogether neglects the high value set upon the young and their impulses throughout the play—especially in the last two acts. At the end no *account* is taken of profit and loss, but all the data are there for anyone who wants to reckon up. Sixteen years have been

VI

The last-minute mating of Camillo and Paulina provides a distraction, a change of emphasis, and a change of tone. With the light-hearted, indulgent approval one accords to unpremeditated weddings at the end of a comedy we note how appropriate it is to unite two old people so similar in worth and dramatic function, and how fitting that the hymeneals should include three generations. The reuniting in marriage of Leontes and Hermione is caught up in the prevailing comedy spirit, embraced in a stock comedy situation. There is no talk now of miracle or mystery. 'It is requir'd / You do awake your faith', Paulina told Leontes, and he seemed to help thereby to give life to his wife's statue. But now fifty lines later he thinks only of how mistaken he has been in ever believing Hermione to have died at all. 'I saw her', he says,

> As I thought, dead; and have in vain said many
> A prayer upon her grave.[1]

We already know from Hermione herself that she never suffered physical death. She 'preserv'd' herself, she told us (= kept in existence), hoping that Perdita was 'in being' (= preserv'd, 124). But Leontes' statement is bald and mundane in contrast, taking account neither of divine dispensation nor of the restorative power of love, but only of the evidence of sense. It is, however, thrown out with an air of gay unconcern; Leontes has no grievance, no feeling of deprivation or deception. That fact, coupled with the parenthetical way in which it is slipped in, shows how little importance Shakespeare is concerned to ascribe to the passage.

And yet he does slip it in. Why? At a similar point in other

---

[1] I.e., her grave being empty, she could not benefit from his prayers. Obviously we must beware of confusing these prayers with Leontes' other spiritual exercises. These prayers have been said 'in vain' as far as Hermione is concerned, and it is of Hermione that he is thinking: those others are not here in question.

---

lost, sixteen years of disseverance (154), but so far as sorrow can ever be swallowed up in joy it is swallowed up here; the children and their heaven-directed happiness are a visible presence, compensating for the unspoken loss of Mamillius: the mood is one of spiritual richness not poverty.

plays Pericles wonders 'How this dead queen re-lives', and Belarius and his supposed sons ask one another 'Is not this boy reviv'd from death?' (*Per.* V, ii, 164, *Cym.* V, v, 120). But they do not know what the audience knows: they think Thaisa and Imogen to be dead; we know them to be alive; our understanding may be enriched by experiencing at second hand their sense of wonder. The reverse is the case here. We and Leontes have been virtually at one, almost equally mystified until the coming down of the statue. The dramatist seems momentarily to treat him therefore at this point as a representative spectator, brought to understand that on the matter-of-fact level there is no mystery. (Leontes' reference to Florizel 'whom, *heavens directing* / Is troth-plight to your daughter' (150) reminds us that more levels of understanding than one are at the same time open to the same spectator.) Shakespeare does this momentarily so as not to dispel the effects already achieved; and he does it in the conventional end-of-comedy context of rapid uncritical resolution so that the good faith of Paulina (and, through her, of Hermione herself) may not be in question. How Paulina found Hermione is to be questioned, and Polixenes has yet to learn where Hermione has lived, but not within the limits of the play. The 'grave and good Paulina' is for Leontes 'Good Paulina' (151) to the end.

Leontes' *obiter dictum* and the light comedy context fit one another perfectly, for they have a common purpose: to prepare for our return to the world of every day by lowering the tone of the play world and reducing its glamour. This is a frequent concern of Shakespeare's at the end of a comedy. An actor comes forward and announces, 'The King's a beggar, now the play is done', or

> If we shadows have offended,
> Think but this, and all is mended,
> That you have but slumber'd here
> While these visions did appear.

Prospero drowns his book and returns to his dukedom: his project was to please the audience, and he must be released from the magic of the stage by the sound of their applause. Similarly with *The Winter's Tale*. It takes all sorts to make an audience, some prone to nearly total engagement in the action, others to varying degrees of aloofness. None must be allowed to think either that something supernatural has happened on the stage or that an

131

unsuccessful attempt has been made to lead him to suppose that it has.

It may be thought that it would have been more effective to leave the question where Paulina left it, and to ask the audience to be content with the knowledge that, fantastic though it may seem, Hermione is alive, and not to inquire further. This is where Northrop Frye (pp. 126f.) thinks Shakespeare did in fact leave it.[1] It is, as he rightly says, as hard to believe that Paulina had been keeping the live Hermione concealed from Leontes all this time as that 'the new Hermione has her origin in Giulio Romano's chisel'; and so, he concludes, 'perhaps we had better stop trying to believe things and simply look at what is in front of us, which is a dramatic exhibition of death and revival'. Agreed—so long as that *is* what is in front of us. But once Hermione speaks we can no longer look on unquestioningly, for then the situation has changed and we have entered the realm of factual explanation.

The point is crucial. The scene has two parts, mystification and resolution, one passing into the other in the lines that separate Hermione's revival from her recovering the power of speech. While the stage magic of the statue engrosses us our critical faculties are dormant. As the sense of wonder fades they start working again, and Shakespeare seeks to satisfy (or appear to satisfy) our scruples, even the most mundane.

VII

This being the case, it may be asked, why any mystery at all? Why the statue? Why not manage the complication and unravelling of the plot on the lines of *Much Ado about Nothing*?[2] To put it

---

[1] Cf. Wilson Knight (pp. 125f.): 'The poet carefully refuses to elucidate the mystery on the plane of plot-realism. . . . We are not, in fact, to search for answers on this plane at all: the poet himself does not know them'. Now that we understand ll. 125ff. this position is not fully tenable.

[2] The corresponding stages in *Much Ado* IV and V are worth recalling. First, Hero's swoon, briefly mistaken for death, and (as the means to a happy end) given out as such:
Beatrice Why, how now, cousin, wherefore sink you down? . . .
Benedick How doth the lady?
Beatrice   Dead, I think. . . .

bluntly, because *The Winter's Tale* is not about nothing. Though it is no thesis play, it is certainly 'about' a great deal more than *Much Ado*. Events in the two plays may in outline seem very similar: the public calumniation and rejection of wife by husband, her apparent death, the innocent deception conceived and carried through by a character of unimpeachable honesty with the intention of reform and reconcilement, the eventual confrontation and reuniting of husband and wife by a trick. The difference in mood

---

Friar (to Leanato)
        Your daughter here the princes left for dead:
        Let her awhile be secretly kept in,
        And publish it that she is dead indeed; . . .
        Marry, this well carried, shall on her behalf
        Change slander to remorse. . . .
                So will it fare with Claudio. . . .
        Come, lady, die to live. (IV, i, 111–255)
Next, Claudio's remorse and preparedness to make reparation (or rather the light comedy correlatives of these):
Claudio   Choose your revenge yourself:
        Impose me to what penance your invention
        Can lay upon my sin: yet sinn'd I not
        But in mistaking. . . .
Leonato   my brother hath a daughter,
        Almost the copy of my child that's dead, . . .
        Give her the right you should have given her cousin,
        And so dies my revenge. . . .
Claudio I do embrace your offer; and dispose
        For henceforth of poor Claudio. (V, i, 282–305)
Lastly, Hero's return and re-betrothal to Claudio *incognita* (flowing from Claudio's readiness to make amends for her death), with the happy assurance that in the mood of comedy his sin may be accounted nothing and her defamation and 'death' matters of passing consequence:
Friar   Did I not tell you she was innocent?
Leonato So are the prince and Claudio who accus'd her
        Upon the error that you heard debated. . . .
        Well, daughter, . . .
            when I send for you, come hither mask'd. . . .
Claudio Give me your hand: before this holy friar:
        I am your husband, if you like of me.
Hero   And when I liv'd, I was your other wife:
        And when you lov'd, you were my other husband. . . .
        One Hero died defil'd, but I do live,
        And surely as I live, I am a maid. . . .
Leonato She died, my lord, but whiles her slander liv'd.
                                  (V, iv, 1–71)

and conduct, however, is radical. *Much Ado* is palpably a game, and we are in the know. Its world is one where everything *can* be known. Impulse and response can be understood at a glance. They are not deeply felt by the dramatist, not even closely thought out; they are conceived largely in terms of situation and of wit. Claudio accuses Hero and casts her off on the flimsiest evidence in the most public manner possible; yet when her father knows the reason, he thinks Claudio was 'innocent' in so doing. Hero at first feels properly outraged; but her sense of injury is short lived, and instead of thinking herself well rid of the wretch she takes him back with evident satisfaction. The death of the Hero who died defiled is easily forgotten, it seems, in the reflection that she did not deserve to die. Here is the distinction between the two plays: in *The Winter's Tale* the death of Hermione not only matters but is of central importance. Over against Claudio's heartless comedy selfishness, 'yet sinn'd I not / But in mistaking', we place the poignant and inclusive truth of Hermione's 'How will this grieve you: . . . / You scarce can right me throughly, then, to say / You did mistake'. Her attitude is that of a martyr rather than a tragic heroine, but our attitude towards her is little different from that of an audience at a tragedy.

The audience at a tragedy is far more emotionally engaged than the audience at a comedy of contrivance, which, though it may identify itself with the fun makers, is at the same time coolly detached. What Shakespeare needs at the middle of *The Winter's Tale* is the complete involvement of the audience in the emotional and moral facts of the situation, and this would certainly not be achieved by making Paulina say, 'Don't worry: Hermione is not dead; but it'll be for Leontes' better purgation for him to think she is'. Contrivance and tipping the wink are tools of comedy inimical to exploring the more intangible and profound levels of experience. If Shakespeare had used these here he would have had to abandon the hope of high seriousness. To explore the dramatic potentialities of the plot (including the oracle and the challenge of the long time lapse) required some other method; but what method? If the audience is not to be taken into a playwright's confidence must it simply be taken in? Cannot truth be conveyed through a falsehood, or a seeming falsehood be proved a truth?

So much for the central scene of the play. In considering the problem of the present scene it has been necessary to look back on that, because the two are implicitly bound up together. The statue scene is such a magnificent *coup de théâtre* that we take its success to be its own justification, and neglect to ask why it came to be introduced. It seems to be the embodiment of an image which from two-fold evidence we know to have teased Shakespeare's imagination—the sculptured figure of Patience in a graveyard, contemplating death with smiling composure—an attitude closely similar to Hermione's in the trial scene. But what we are concerned with now is the efficient cause, what prompted Shakespeare to devise such a scene for this place; and the technical reason seems to be, to balance and justify in the design of the play Paulina's speech reporting Hermione's death. That is theatrical, calculated to convince the audience absolutely: these qualities must be repeated here. Once Hermione's death is handled in those terms, once its nature is kept a secret from the audience, Paulina cannot be made simply to lead Hermione back alive into her husband's arms—whether from a sixteen-year trance or illness, or like Hero as a substitute for herself ('As like Hermione as is her picture'). The sudden disparity of that, abruptly turning the play into a comedy of contrivance, would expose Paulina's conduct in III, ii, to the retrospective scrutiny of common sense, making her out to be a liar and Hermione a party to an impudent fraud.

Some means of return must therefore be found for Hermione which permits us to reconcile her death and restoration with Paulina's being 'grave and good', something which will rise to the dignity of the occasion not sink it in unseasonable laughter. As in the earlier scene the total involvement of the audience must be secured, and contrivance must be kept out of sight as a great dissipater of concentrated concern (cf. the second halves of *All's Well* and *Measure for Measure*). The use of the statue meets these conditions wonderfully well. A death that is no death—a lie that embodies a truth—is matched and supported by a revival that is no revival—a make-believe statue making believe to come to life, which yet betokens a genuine return to fulness of life and conveys a quality of miracle which appertains to human life itself.[1]

---

[1] The device is turned to incidental advantage in several ways. In the course of the scene Leontes recalls his wooing, and Paulina recalls it too (38, 108): the suggestion is that, participating in Hermione's revival, Leontes now at last, after sixteen years, 'new-woos' his queen, without the embarrassment of inter-communication, for they are infinitely removed from one another, he

VIII

The immediately striking thing about the statue scene, however, is not its dramatic character but its theatricality, the element of excited, awed, engrossed attention which stills for the moment all disposition to reason, question, doubt. This is not a normal case of willing suspension of disbelief, not by any means a typical instance of drama, the art of illusion: as I have suggested, it is much nearer to being a case of enforced belief, of delusion. Ordinarily the conjurer's craft and the playwright's do not overlap: here they do, and for good reason. Only so could the sense of miracle be imparted. Normally we are in the know, and can say loftily with the deluder, 'Lord, what fools these mortals be!' when we see how easily the stage persons are deceived.

But here we do no such thing, for we are deceived ourselves—almost deceived. Clues have already been given suggesting that Hermione may be on the way back to life (V, i) and that the statue may not be all it is supposed to be (V, ii); and in the course of the proceedings here Paulina is significantly anxious to prevent anyone from touching the statue. Some such qualifications of our total engagement the dramatist must make by anticipation, for no matter how good the acting may be the statue may seem to move (as Paulina warns Leontes), may seem indeed more like Hermione than a statue. But that is by no means the same thing as taking us into his confidence. He *wants* us to be possessed by the experience, and he also wants the affair to be, up to a point, capable of rational explanation afterwards. So having laid his clues he exploits the theatrical magic inherent in the situation for all it is worth. And

---

flesh and blood, she stone. The enormous assumption that a living woman could in the circumstances stand insensible to the sight of loved ones does not arise, for the overriding assumption is that she is a statue. Its revival is a piece of theatrical shorthand symbolically comprehending the stages of Hermione's slow recovery. The manner of her calling down and her apparently difficult response indicate her long petrified emotional state and how hard it is for the renewed woman to break herself free of its still confining incrustations. Hermione's silence and Leontes' reluctantly taking her by the hand, touches reminiscent of the *Alcestis*, indicate the transition from walking statue to living woman, and prolong the enveloping sense of awe and mystery.

we are captivated. We allow ourselves to be bemused. The situation is novel and exciting, the conjurer is putting on an excellent show: 'Whether this be / Or not be, I'll not swear', we say, but 'If it be thus to dream, still let me sleep'.

As we have seen, immediately the statue comes down, the stage persons start asking questions for us; and once doubt enters, delusion is turned to illusion: we no longer concede that Hermione was a statue but that she seemed to be one. Up to that critical point in the resolution, when the normal degree of audience participation would not have sufficed, we have by a kind of self-delusion—a quite exceptional order of co-operation— helped the dramatist to 'force a play'.[1] Our near delusion (heightened by the interest of novelty) has served the dramatist's turn in stifling common-sense criticism until Hermione is restored to her husband, with her dignity and Paulina's honesty unimpaired. Her return is then shown to be consistent both with common sense and with a sense of miracle.

No god, no fairy or magician directly takes part in the action. But marvel has been by no means lacking. The fates of Mamillius, Perdita, Antigonus and the mariners have variously shown the participation of the gods in human affairs (V, i, 172, III, iii, 5, V, ii, 71). Hermione has miraculously appeared to Antigonus in a dream, named her child to him and told him where to leave it. Leontes' penitence has been more effective in moving the gods than 'A thousand knees' could have been, 'Ten thousand years together, naked, fasting, / Upon a barren mountain'. Camillo has performed 'almost a miracle'. Leontes' 'saint-like sorrow' and Camillo's wisdom and loyalty are paralleled in other characters too, notably in the self-sacrifice of Antigonus. The miraculous power of Hermione's motherly devotion to direct and preserve, her patience, her confidence, are happily associated with the loyalty, wisdom, piety and medicinable devotion of that other director and preserver, Paulina.

---

[1] As we sit rapt, we do not think of Paulina fixing Hermione up in her niche, instructing her about attitude, reminding her not to move or speak until called upon to do so, and to be quite unresponsive to the sight or voice of anyone but Paulina. To these thoughts we shut our mind, much as we may shut our eyes to things going on in the wings which we may catch sight of from a side box. They are necessary pieces of carpentry, not part of the experience designed by the dramatist.

It is altogether fitting, therefore, that the last scene of all should overtop the rest in presenting the sense of miracle, and especially of human miracle. What happens in V, ii, is wonderful enough: the branch that had been lopped from the tree is restored alive and jointed to it; but what happens in V, iii, is more wonderful still: one of the dual stems, dead many years, has after revived and been jointed to its fellow. This is the occasion of a prolonged display of love, contrition and admiration by Leontes, and it is strongly suggested that the wonderful reanimation of Hermione is partly dependent on his wanting and deserving it so much.[1] For her part the wonder is rather that Perdita has been preserved, and it is to her confident hope of this that she ascribes her own preservation. Between them they have knit up the family once more and, 'heavens directing', supplied the irreparable gap. At the back of all there is the direction of the gods, most clearly indicated in the oracle and its fulfilment; but their will is not performed without human co-operation.

The final note, we must not forget, is that of urbane, social comedy. The last act, for all its wonder, can join hands at the end with the initial mood of the first. The play does not remain on the Mount of Contemplation, but returns renewed in spirit to the world of every day.

[1] Leontes in his ardour and excitement reminds us of Cordelia in the reconciliation scene (*K.L.* IV, vii). Unheard by the loved one (Hermione is a statue, Lear asleep) both can speak out with a warmth and depth of love hardly possible for them to voice in other circumstances.

Epilogue

I

Before we draw together the strings of the argument we may briefly relate our play, in point of theme and mood, to others of Shakespeare's, and to contemporary work of Beaumont and Fletcher. As has often been remarked, they could not have written Shakespeare's Romances, and he could not have written theirs; for Shakespeare worked with the older values and standards of conduct in mind. Leontes' sudden jealousy is unique in *The Winter's Tale*. He stands out as the victim of a moral disease, because the rest of his world is morally sound. Philaster's jealousy is also sudden, but it is not to be regarded as a disease. His responses to the situation are of the same kind as other characters' responses. All who hear the allegations against Arethusa immediately believe them without question—all except Bellario, who has personal reasons for knowing them to be false. Moral stability is not for them the normal thing: they do not naturally expect it of her. The play is an enclosed moral world. Philaster's flawed and erratic sense of honour is not the subject of adverse comment within it. The Country Fellow is a *rusticus ex machina* briefly introduced to wound Philaster, not so that we may think any the worse of the hero for striking a woman. Consistency of moral judgement, or of normal emotional response, is not required of the audience any more than it is of the characters. When Arethusa's relations with Bellario are under suspicion we are not expected to feel how much harm Philaster must be doing to Arethusa, to himself, and to their relationship by so misjudging her—none, indeed, is harmed at all —but only how piquant the situation is, what a delightful train of interesting situations is made to flow from it, and what promise of a surprising dénouement it contains.

Noting that in the survival of Hermione 'we have a unique Shakespearian instance of a major secret . . . being kept from the audience as well as the characters', Clifford Leech (p. 156) remarks that 'there is an obvious link here with the revelation of Bellario's identity in *Philaster*'. What is the nature of this link? Does it mean anything more than that the climate of the drama was favourable to the use of such a *coup de théâtre* as the statue scene? As a theatrical novelty the case of Bellario must indeed have attracted Shakespeare's interest. But can we say that it prompted him to treat the death of Hermione as he did?

The two cases are similar in that in both the final discovery resolves the complication and makes possible the happy union of hero and heroine. But they are also profoundly different. When Bellario turns out to be a girl it does not involve her good faith or the good faith of any other character. It is not a material change: it does not alter the original relationship of Bellario, Arethusa and Philaster. For all the difference the revelation makes to Bellario she might as well still be a boy. Throughout the play she is sexless devotion. In her disguise she has no hope of marrying Philaster (who is too high-born for her), and out of it she will not marry any other man. At the end she is to remain in the service of Arethusa who 'cannot be jealous' of her. The discovery proves Arethusa's innocence in a novel, piquant way, and as it is provoked by the threat of stripping and torture it may sketch a sadistic thrill; but it is patently a device to effect the dénouement, not an event of major consequence.

The case of Hermione is quite different: it involves the *bona fides* of the entire play. If she has not in any sense been dead, we have been deceived in the play's most strongly emphasized datum, that Paulina is the embodiment of trust and honour. If Paulina has lied she has lied to the audience, and that is the unforgivable sin. Whether one character may deceive another in Shakespeare without losing credit will depend on circumstances, but on no account may he deceive the audience concerning a matter of consequence. Even when we know of his deception from the context, he will sometimes turn aside to tell us of it, usually to excuse himself. Examples are Imogen's direct address to the audience, 'If I do lie and do/ No harm by it, though the gods hear, I hope / They'll pardon it', and Pisanio's resolution in soliloquy of his perplexities: 'Wherein I am false, I am honest; not true, to be true' (*Cym.* IV, ii, 377; IV, iii, 42). Camillo's later intrigues are another case in point. He arranges Florizel's elopement with Perdita, schools him in what lies to tell when they get to

Leontes' court, and then informs Polixenes, so that he and Polixenes may go in pursuit. Florizel, hearing of their speedy arrival in Sicilia, is understandably shocked: 'Camillo has betray'd me; / Whose honour and whose honesty till now / Endur'd all weathers' (V, i, 192). But when at the end of the play Camillo's 'worth and honesty' are praised, we in the audience warmly approve, for he has kept faith with us and punctually informed us of his motives and intentions (IV, iv, 509, 662). Paulina, on the other hand, never explains herself. The inference is that she has nothing to explain, that she has practised no deception. It is not intended that at any point we should doubt her good faith.

That being granted, Hermione's revival is no mere end-of-play thrill, no mere happy solution of a seemingly insoluble problem, but part of the groundwork. Her death and her revival are two hinged events. They are conducted at so much higher a pitch of theatrical and dramatic consequence than the discovery of Bellario's sex that it is hard even grudgingly to concede that the germ of the idea of this double deception-that-is-no-deception is traceable to that example. There was a growing taste for masque-like elements in the theatres—to which the theophanies in *Pericles* and *Cymbeline*, the 'saltiers' at the sheep shearing, and the masque of spirits in *The Tempest* all bear witness—and to this taste the spectacle of a statue brought to life was to be highly agreeable. Fundamental, however, is its dramatic intention. In this scene the quintessence of the other Romances receives expression. The moving statue, an image of great theatrical force, evokes a sense of wonder which closely identifies the scene with their drift and purpose: the recognition of the miracle of life and the restorative power of the human spirit. That affinity is manifestly paramount.

Time the Chorus, far from parading *The Winter's Tale* as keeping up with the Beaumonts and Fletchers, presents it as old fashioned (IV, i, 13). Shakespeare may indeed have had Beaumont and Fletcher in mind when he wrote of 'th'freshest things now reigning' and 'The glistering of this present': their smart up-to-date manner was not for him, nor their superficiality of tone. That he took an interest in their plays need not be doubted for a moment, but as an influence on Shakespeare they must be accounted comparatively insignificant.[1] While Fletcher was writing

[1] During the closure of the London theatres in 1609 (see Appendix II) he and Beaumont and Fletcher may have been thrown together. Before that the

The Faithful Shepherdess, verbal and rhythmical echoes of *A Midsummer Night's Dream* intruded upon his work. Likewise in writing Ariel's part in *The Tempest* Shakespeare allowed verbal and rhythmical echoes of Fletcher's Satyr in *The Faithful Shepherdess* to slip in. But further specific connexions between the two plays are harder to pin down. Clifford Leech (pp. 158f.) sees Shakespeare in Fletcher's debt, because '*The Tempest* and *The Faithful Shepherdess* both have at their centre a human being with magical control over the play's events'. But Paulina may be said to have corresponding though not magical control over her play's events: her apparent magic with the statue could easily have turned Shakespeare's thoughts to a play of true magic. Again, if we see a resemblance between Clorin and Prospero in their possessing a kind of god-like power we must remember also Cerimon, who holds that virtue and cunning make 'a man a god'. Through him the heavens work, so that he can perform a 'great miracle': 'Reverend sir', says Pericles,

> The gods can have no mortal officer
> More like a god than you.
>
> *(Per.* III, ii, 27, 96, V, iii, 58)

And then there is *A Midsummer Night's Dream*. Oberon is not, like Prospero, human, but they are both princes who have at their command beings not dissimilar in nature, through whom in very similar ways they control events. In fairy comedy man does not need power over airy spirits: it is fun that their actions should be unpredictable, for it is axiomatic that they can do no lasting harm. But in the world of tragi-comedy such power, if available, should certainly be under beneficent human control, for there man stands in danger from man. From this point of view *The Tempest* can be

---

younger men had written only for boy actors, but in that year they were quite possibly at work on *Philaster* for performance by the King's Servants. Shakespeare, probably engaged on *Cymbeline* at the time and perhaps asked for advice about *Philaster*, could have been shown a draft of their play. This would explain what look like instances of reciprocal influence in these two works: *Cymbeline* seems at V, ii, 2–6 to echo *Phil.* IV, iii, 105, whereas in the spate of forgiveness at the end of *Philaster* the influence no doubt operates the other way. The composition of *The Winter's Tale* came later. At IV, iv, 129–132 there is a reminiscence of *Phil.* IV, iv, 2–6, but this hardly amounts to evidence of influence.

seen as the tragi-comic correlative of *A Midsummer Night's Dream*.

II

If then the makings of the idea of Prospero and his airy spirit are present in other plays of Shakespeare's own, can anything similar be said of the statue scene in *The Winter's Tale*? Reference has already been made to Marina's likeness (and Viola's 'sister's') to a sculpture of Patience in a graveyard, in calm and hopeful endurance outfacing sorrow and suffering. And there is also Imogen, no statue even in similitude, but a wife dead to her husband and seeming to him and others to return from death at the end of the play. It may well be that the statue scene represents the imaginative fusion of these two conceptions, the woman like Patience on a monument and the woman dead to her husband yet eventually restored to him.

What distinguishes the scene is the use of metaphor not simile: the woman is not likened to a statue but identified with one. The device expresses the paradox that she is both dead and alive. Thaisa briefly looks like death, and for two acts is 'supposed dead' (*Per.* V, iii, 35); but before going into her long seclusion she explains her action to us: it is due to chance separation from her beloved husband (III, iv, 8); it by no means betokens numbing ill-usage or estrangement. Imogen also suffers seeming death but does not disappear from the action; in her case too we are in no doubt about what actually happens. Hence the repeated assertions towards the end that Imogen has indeed been dead (*Cym.* V, v, 120, 123, 126, 259) cannot take full possession of our minds. They seem to indicate a need for some mode of metaphoric statement such as we find in *The Winter's Tale*, but they lack symbolic justification. For though Imogen, unlike Thaisa, is the victim of her husband's folly and cruelty, neither she nor her love for him is deeply injured in consequence: nothing in her has 'died' through her ill-treatment. Thus Imogen's part in *Cymbeline* may have predisposed Shakespeare to seek, for another play, a plot which would involve the death, at once seeming and actual, of a wife through her husband's cruelty, her consequent absence from the action until he had expiated the wrongs he had done her, some degree of uncertainty in the audience regarding the facts (to accord with their ambiguous nature), and, finally, some means of resolution on the metaphorical or symbolical plane.

It is worth noting in this connexion that in several respects the case of Hermione is the case of Imogen more deeply felt into by the dramatist. In *Cymbeline* III, iv, Imogen, prepared to die at her husband's command, grieves to think what pangs he will be caused by the memory of her whom now he tortures:

> I grieve myself
> To think, when thou shalt be disedg'd by her
> That now thou tirest on, how thy memory
> Will then be pang'd by me.

These words, addressed to the husband in her mind's eye, are, it would seem, a first sketch for Hermione directly confronting her husband:

> How will this grieve you,
> When you shall come to clearer knowledge, that
> You thus have publish'd me! Gentle my lord,
> You scarce can right me throughly, then, to say
> You did mistake.

That passage is written out of a far keener comprehension of the woman's grief and wounded honour, out of a full sense of the unbroken unity of husband and wife in their separation and yet of the seeming finality of that separation. Again, when it appears that Pisanio wishes not to kill her but to give it out that she is dead Imogen is at a loss:

> What shall I do the while? where bide? how live?
> Or in my life what comfort, when I am
> Dead to my husband?

Here she anticipates the thought but not the poignancy of Hermione's response to Leontes' words, 'Look for no less than death':

> Sir, spare your threats:
> The bug which you would fright me with, I seek.
> To me life can be no commodity;
> The crown and comfort of my life, your favour,
> I do give lost, for I do feel it gone,
> But know not how it went.

Once more Imogen's speech lacks the immediacy of direct con-frontation. It is in comparison rationally thought out. She is dead to her husband because he has wanted her dead and will believe her dead, not because his treatment of her has made her emotion-ally dead to him. She has hysterically sought to make Pisanio strike with his sword 'The innocent mansion of my love, my heart';

> Fear not [she encouraged him]: 'tis empty of all things but grief:
> Thy master is not there, who was indeed
> The riches of it.

Her words suggest something of Hermione's situation but not her character. Imogen stagily demands to be killed because of a strained and formal sense of duty, to show her wifely obedience. Hermione in one part of her mind is content to die because emotionally she is already dead; but in another part of her mind she determines to preserve herself and smile extremity out of act, because the oracle gives hope.

III

That 'pitee renneth sone in gentil herte', that 'gentil mercy oghte to passen right'—cardinal doctrine of Christian chivalry—was well known to the Elizabethans through Chaucerian and other romance. We find it in Greene's *Pandosto*:

> And if she had faulted [say Pandosto's lords, interceding on the queen's behalf], yet it were more honourable to pardon with mercy than to punish with extremity, and more kingly to be commended of pity than accused of rigour. (p. 193)

Tamora cites it like a copy-book maxim—

> Sweet mercy is nobility's true badge—

along with another to similar effect—

> Wilt thou draw near the nature of the gods?
> Draw near them then in being merciful.
> (*Tit. And.* I, i, 117)

The thought of those two maxims combines to form the ground-work of Portia's 'quality of mercy' speech. That speech embodies the characteristic Shakespearean opposition to what is 'strain'd'

—Lear speaks of 'strain'd pride' (*K.L.* I, i, 172)—and what is narrowly legalistic—e.g. in Shylock, in Egeus, and in Angelo.

Measure for Measure well shows—in places—the clear strain of Christian idealism in Shakespeare's thought. Isabella's implicit forgiveness of Angelo in pleading for his life, and her earlier appeal to him—

> O, think on that:
> And mercy then will breathe within your lips
> Like man new made— (II, ii, 77)

anticipate a fundamental attitude of the Romances, seen in Posthumus's sentence on Iachimo—

> The power that I have on you is to spare you—
> (*Cym.* V, v, 418)

in Hermione's qualification, in wishing that her father could see the flatness of her misery,

> —yet with eyes
> Of pity, not revenge!— (*W.T.* III, ii, 122)

and in Prospero's noble treatment of his enemies—

> the rarer action is
> In virtue than in vengeance: they being penitent,
> The sole drift of my purpose doth extend
> Not a frown further. Go release them, Ariel.
> (*Temp.* V, i, 27)

Yet impressive as Isabella's image of redemption and regeneration undoubtedly is ('mercy then will breathe within your lips / Like man new made'), the range of correspondence between her play and the Romances is limited. Concern with two generations at once, the strength of the family bond, loss of dear ones, miraculous preservation, wonderful reunion—there is nothing of all that in *Measure for Measure*.

It is in *King Lear* that the spirit that informs the Romances first makes itself fully felt. In the reconciliation scene, to the accompaniment of music, Cordelia's kiss brings the medicine of restoration to repair her father's violent harms. This is a scene of forgiveness and benediction. It presents a harmony of opposites, age and youth, experience and daring, destructive violence and healing love, and final reunion after long and painful separation, almost as though from death ('You do me wrong to take me out of the grave', says Lear from his imaginary wheel of fire, thinking Cordelia a soul in bliss).

King Lear does not end with the reconciliation scene. The Romances do. They are at once abstractions upon *Lear* and extensions of it.[1] In them the spirit of mercy can conclude the play. Leontes, unlike Pandosto, gets his wife back. Posthumus forgives Iachimo, and Cymbeline outgoes him in submitting to Caesar, although he is the victor. The emphasis, that is to say, is on heart not head, on forgiveness not condemnation, on disregard of self-interest for the sake of others. In *King Lear* that emphasis is certainly present too, not only in the reconciliation scene but as a continuous undercurrent throughout: in the selfless loyalty, the 'love' (IV, ii, 96), of Kent, the Fool, Edgar and Gloucester, and in the humanity of the First Servant. The regenerate Lear intends that whenever Cordelia asks for blessing he will kneel down and ask forgiveness for himself; she redeems nature, the Gentleman says, from the general curse of the Fall, re-enacted by her wicked sisters; and in honour of her self-sacrifice ('For thee, oppressed

---

[1] In their world, for instance, there are no unkind daughters; but none, not even Marina, can be of such unspeakable comfort to her father as Cordelia is to Lear. Lear is more keenly aware of the physical oneness of the family than Hermione herself; and the ideal harmony of its parts has gone far worse awry for him:

> Is it not as this mouth should tear this hand
> For lifting food to't? (*K.L.* III, iv, 15)
> But yet thou art my flesh, my blood, my daughter;
> Or rather a disease that's in my flesh,
> Which I must needs call mine. (II, iv, 224)

At moments of restoration in the Romances the talk of 'flesh of thy flesh, Thaisa' and 'my flesh, my child' (*Per.* V, iii, 46, *Cym.* V, v, 264), is flat indeed in comparison.

On the other hand, the image of the tree whose branches, if severed, 'perforce must wither / And come to deadly use' (*K.L.* IV, ii, 35) is inverted in the more fortunate and positive world of the Romances. There conjugal love bears a full part in sustaining and renewing the family tree. It is while Posthumus, asleep, speaks to his wife in silence, as he puts it (*Cym.* V, iv, 28)— to the wife he believes he has had killed—that the ghosts of his dead parents and brothers appear to him and intercede on his behalf to Jupiter, who delivers his prophecy. This amounts, like the oracle in *The Winter's Tale*, to a promise of family reunion: branches dead many years shall revive and be jointed to the old stock.

king, am I cast down'), the gods invert order by burning incense
(V, ii, 20). But that is not the dominant emphasis—rather that

> men
> Are as the time is: to be tender-minded
> Does not become a sword,

and that when love fails barbarity reigns. Unless the gods execute
summary justice

> Humanity must perforce prey on itself
> Like monsters of the deep.

In *King Lear* facts are, for the most part, hard and unyielding.
When the king enters 'with Cordelia in his arms', he knows 'She's
dead as earth', and she is. When Arviragus enters 'with Imogen
dead, bearing her in his arms', the brothers are mistaken: she is
not dead. 'This feather stirs', cries Lear, momentarily deceived:

> she lives! if it be so,
> It is a chance which does redeem all sorrows
> That ever I have felt.

Leontes gets that chance: Hermione lives: all his sorrows are
redeemed. Pericles gets it:

> This, this: no more, you gods! your present kindness
> Makes my past miseries sports.

King Lear does not get it. Cordelia is dead as earth.

'She lives! if it be so . . .': it is an expression of hope only, and
the hope is vain. The fact, as Lear reiterates, is that 'she's gone for
ever', will

> come no more,
> Never, never, never, never, never.

'If this be so', says Cymbeline—that Imogen is alive—

> the gods do mean to strike me
> To death with mortal joy.

It is so, but they do not strike him to death. In the grim world of
Lear it is otherwise: when Gloucester finds his child alive his
heart,

> 'Twixt two extremes of passion, joy and grief,
> Burst smilingly.

As for King Lear himself, on the point of death he once more hopes against hope:

> Do you see this? Look on her! Look her lips,
> Look there, look there.

But it is no use. His child is dead, and so, at that moment, is he. Paulina, in contrast, hoping against hope, acts in harmony with heaven's will in so doing (*W.T.* V, i, 35–46). That Leontes' lost child will be found is as monstrous to human reason as that her dead husband should break his grave and return; and yet she hopes. In the event we see her to be doubly justified in doubting the verdict of reason: Leontes gets back both child and wife.

At times of disaster, suffering and death may seem the only realities. But there must be life for there to be death, and the power to suffer for there to be suffering. Without these positive and negative forces in conflict there could be no tragedy. The full statement of reality is life *and* death, static fact *and* mobile potentiality. To this dichotomy the Romances are likewise very much alive, but their ultimate bias is where possible towards resolution of seeming contrariety and discord. In the tragedies faith and hope and love do survive as an earnest of future well-being, but the emphasis is on their vulnerability, and on the power of evil to destroy. In the Romances evil can still threaten and destroy, but its power is limited, held in check, transcended finally by the recuperative powers of life. The ingredients of tragedy are present, but they work in the framework of comedy. Cymbeline's queen, Cloten, the conspirators in *The Tempest*—their evil is relatively ineffectual: Cornelius, the two boys, and Ariel are at hand to see to that. Leontes in his possession, though dreadful, is not to be compared with the women who turn monsters. When the gods strike at his injustice, killing his son, he instantly comes to his senses and is capable of right moral judgement, even against himself, whereas Cornwall and the wicked sisters, scenting danger, spring to more vindictive cruelties.

Shakespeare's Romances are the comedies of a man who having written the tragedies is not prepared to cut the material of life to the customary measure of comedy. In them he takes a broader and deeper view of sin and death, nobility and promise, than comedy customarily allows, and exhibits a larger indulgence and high seriousness in dealing with them.

IV

> Thy life's a miracle. . . .
> Think that the clearest gods, that make them honours
> Of men's impossibilities, have preserv'd thee.

These words might stand as an epigraph for all the Romances. They are spoken by Edgar in *King Lear* to sustain his blinded father, whom he has just saved by a trick from committing suicide. He speaks them not in further pious deception but as comfortable doctrine, as a perfectly just interpretation of the occurrence. Shakespeare has in mind Christ's answer to the disciples' question, 'Who then can be saved?'—'With men this is impossible; but with God all things are possible.'[1] Characteristically Shakespeare thinks of salvation in earthly not heavenly terms, and of the miraculous power of the gods as at work in our own world.

It would be a fitting epigraph because of the many instances of seemingly miraculous preservation that the Romances contain. But out of their context Edgar's words fail to convey what in their dramatic setting is plain to see, that in the performance of such 'impossibilities' the gods act through men. This point is given prominence in the Romances.

> Now do I long to hear how you were found,

says Pericles when Thaisa is discovered,

> How possibly preserv'd; and who to thank,
> Besides the gods, for this great miracle.

[1] Already in *All's Well* Shakespeare is occupied with this idea. The character, indeed the whole story, of Helena is founded upon it. This is particularly evident in her first interview with the King, when she offers him her medical aid which has 'something in't / More than [her] father's skill':

Helena　It is not so with him that all things knows
　　　　As 'tis with us that square our guess by shows. . . .
　　　　Of heaven, not me, make an experiment. . . .
King　　Methinks in thee some blessed spirit doth speak
　　　　His powerful sound within an organ weak:
　　　　And what impossibility would slay
　　　　In common sense, sense saves another way.

(II, i, 152–81)

The answer is

> Lord Cerimon, my lord; this man
> Through whom the gods have shown their power.

Prospero tells Miranda,

> O a cherubin
> Thou wast that did preserve me. Thou didst smile,
> Infused with a fortitude from heaven.

'How came we ashore?' she asks. 'By Providence divine', he replies. But Providence used human agency: 'Holy Gonzalo' was their 'true preserver'. Paulina is in similar case. She alone can decipher the oracle as giving hope, and so becomes Hermione's true preserver. Camillo unknowingly leads the missing heir safely home; but it is Paulina who, staunch in her faith in the divine Apollo, deliberately and energetically keeps the way open for that event, confident that the oracle will be fulfilled, and that the gods can achieve what to our human reason is impossible.

V

The Winter's Tale starts with a normal condition of civilized existence, based on the ideal of the growth of friendship, and delight in the rising generation. Suddenly this state of affairs is shattered by Leontes' multiple breach of the trust on which civilized society depends. Other ideals emerge and stand firm, however. Hermione's sense of family honour and of responsibility to her descendants, Paulina's instinct to protect and reform, her conviction that the gods will have performed their secret purposes, Florizel's twofold ideal of personal honour and loyalty to his beloved—these, added to the self-sacrifice of Antigonus and the not disinterested devotion of Camillo, sustain, preserve and cure, and help eventually to make good most of the loss and damage. In that process Leontes' long performance of his own compensating ideal of constant penitence is fundamental. The benevolent participation of the heavens is axiomatic, but their purposes are achieved not by men's sitting back and waiting but by their active though unwitting collaboration. Hermione, fortified by Paulina's hope, preserves herself; Leontes' tears are, though he does not know it, tears of re-creation (III, ii, 240).

That is the play in outline. It remains to show how the part of the hero gives a special quality to its effectiveness, and more particularly to the effectiveness of the last act.

The Winter's Tale is peculiar among the Romances not in the evil and suffering that it contains but in identifying its hero as their source and agent. This gives the play complexity and depth of interest; but it also involves a considerable danger. The hero becomes despicable before our eyes. He becomes a scourge to himself and to all he holds most dear. His ugly fantasies, his cheap and clever équivoques, the disgusting, delighted pain he causes himself, linger disturbingly in the memory, no less than his demented cruelties to others. Can a man like this, a man we remember with such strong disfavour, regain his standing as the noble hero of romance?

At first sight the construction of the play would seem to be altogether against his doing so. It allows three acts (or the better part of three acts) to display Leontes at full length as in the highest degree contemptible and unpleasant, and utterly unworthy of his wife. And it gives no opportunity for us to see him during his long purgation, and not a great deal after it, so that it seems very doubtful whether the balance of sympathy can possibly be redressed in time. To be sure, when we learn of his purgation we are, after a scene of youth and love, prepared to look indulgently upon him. But can we warm towards him? Can we actively like and admire him? To make us do just that must be the business of the last act.

In meeting this challenge Shakespeare sharpens the focus of the structure he inherited from Greene, clarifying the tripartite movement and introducing a thesis-antithesis-synthesis relationship between the parts. Just before the initial movement of the play ends 'things dying' yield place to 'things new born', and this gives promise of an antithetical movement to come. Accordingly in the fourth act, where, following the pattern of *Pandosto*, Florizel and Perdita displace Leontes and Hermione, the lovers introduce as leading motifs forthright virtue, acceptance and preservation, in place of doubt, sin, rejection and destruction: they represent daring youth in opposition and contrast to repressive age. On his return in Act V, Leontes resumes his central place, but his world is now enriched, and he is enlarged, by the presence of the young: the virtues of the two generations are in harmony, mutually supporting. Leontes' expiation of his sin is the efficient cause of Perdita's return and hence of Hermione's. Even the finality of death seems relaxed, for besides the 'she that was lost' whom we know to be alive, Hermione, also lost—irrecoverably, we had supposed—is restored almost as by a miracle.

The last act is tight packed. It has a great deal to do and little space to do it in. It has rapidly to reinstate the main thesis figure, Leontes, bring the antithesis into relationship with the thesis, and then introduce the synthesis. For this purpose it divides itself into three scenes—interrelated, like the movements of the play itself.

In Scene i Leontes is seen as regenerated. He is successively the humble penitent, content to leave the issue to Paulina and the gods; the gracious host; and the noble patron of honourable love in distress. We note his spontaneous admiration of youth and honour, and his ready willingness to help and protect it even when, as it appears, the young man intends to marry beneath him. In this transitionary scene father and daughter, unknown to one another, meet on terms of mutual trust and admiration. This prepares us for the recognition scene, in which our excitement that the oracle is fulfilled is stimulated by the spectacle of the gentlemen's excitement on the stage, and yet we are saved from too anxious concern about the reunion by seeing it (as already accomplished) with the gentlemen's elegant detachment. Eased thus into happy relationship first with the regenerate king and now with the regenerate father we are ready for active involvement on behalf of the regenerate husband. In the final scene he is first the venerating lover, eager to embrace his dead wife's statue, then the awestruck husband, doubtfully embracing his wife so miraculously restored, and finally the gay and assured sovereign, husband, friend and father, including all about him, old and young, in the ritual of unification.

The whole act, with its varied and unforced emphases concerning Leontes—its easy postulation of a sensitive and generous nature, its unquestioning assumption that he enjoys the sympathy and good will of all—is a brilliant response to the difficulties and dangers it seemed inherently to contain.

Further Notes on *Pandosto* and *The Winter's Tale*

A

Leontes' Jealousy (*W.T.* I, ii)

Pandosto is introduced as a model of kingly virtue, fortunate and feared in war, loved in peace, of 'bountiful courtesy' towards his friends and subjects. He and his wife are 'linked together in perfect love'. When Egistus comes to visit them

> Bellaria, who in her time was the flower of courtesy, willing to show how unfeignedly she loved her husband by his friend's entertainment, used him likewise so familiarly that her countenance bewrayed how her mind was affected towards him, oftentimes coming herself into his bed chamber to see that nothing should be amiss to mislike him. This honest familiarity increased daily more and more betwixt them; for Bellaria, noting in Egistus a princely and bountiful mind, adorned with sundry and excellent qualities, and Egistus, finding in her a virtuous and courteous disposition, there grew such a secret uniting of their affections, that the one could not well be without the company of the other. (p. 185)

In consequence, 'a certain melancholy passion entering the mind of Pandosto drave him into sundry and doubtful thoughts', which, 'a long time smothering in his stomach', grew into a flaming jealousy, so that he watched and measured all their actions, misconstrued 'their too private familiarity', and judged that Egistus had played him false.

All this, with earlier talk of the perfection of Pandosto's son and recollection of the boyhood friendship and pastimes of the two kings—can we say that Shakespeare has changed it in any essential point? He uses dramatic economy, of course, and assigns the action to the last day of Polixenes' visit instead of the first and many later days, but the detail and its sequence are not significantly different.

In both versions the actions of the queen and the visiting king are presented in terms of fine courtly attitude and sentiment, high minded and noble. In transferring the events of the first day of Egistus's visit to the last day of Polixenes', Shakespeare follows Greene so closely that he even adapts a commonplace account of the everyday courtesies of welcome:

> Pandosto . . . embraced [Egistus] very lovingly, protesting that nothing in the world could have happened more acceptable to him than his coming, wishing his wife to welcome his old friend and acquaintance. . . .

In this seemingly casual statement the natural inclusion of the wife in the civilities of the occasion is the romance-writer's way of giving early prominence to her part in the story, for the passage continues, referring to Bellaria:

> . . . who, to show how she liked him whom her husband loved, entertained him with such familiar courtesy as Egistus perceived himself to be very well welcome. (p. 185)

Correspondingly in Shakespeare, on the intended departure of Polixenes, Leontes urges his friend to stay longer and, when he protests that he cannot, asks his wife to try and make him change his mind; and this is the dramatist's means of turning our attention to Hermione (her reply is her first speech in the play) and of displaying her innocent 'familiar courtesy'. That leads directly to her husband's murmur, 'At my request he would not'. This murmur corresponds to Pandosto's 'secret mistrust', which, increased by suspicion, grows at last into a flaming jealousy.[1]

---

[1] These, the next stages in Leontes' disease, Shakespeare mainly develops independently of Greene (ll. 87–185). In two passages, however, he still has *Pandosto* in mind. The first comes at the onset of Leontes' active suspicion:

> This entertainment
> May a free face put on. . . .
> But to be paddling palms and pinching fingers,
>   . . . O, that is entertainment
> My bosom likes not, nor my brows. (111)

This, with its double mention of 'entertainment', seems to hark back to the double use of the word at the beginning of *Pandosto*, where seeming ambiguity in Bellaria's behaviour towards Egistus is implied: she

Recognizing all this, can we doubt that Shakespeare intends to follow Greene in the earlier part of the scene also, and to show Leontes there not as a jealous man playing a part to gather evidence, but like Pandosto a man of bountiful courtesy linked in perfect love with his wife (the flower of courtesy) and genuinely delighted with his friend's company?

B

The Winter's Tale II, iii

Though half of the scene is dominated by Paulina, a character of Shakespeare's invention, much of its detail is suggested by Greene's narrative. There (pp. 191–3), Egistus being too powerful and too strongly allied to defeat in war, Pandosto was content 'to put up [i.e. sheathe] a manifest injury with peace'. When he sent Bellaria to prison he determined that she 'should pay for all at an unreasonable price'; when he knew that she was with child 'he could take no rest until he might mitigate his choler with a just revenge'; and when he heard that the child was born he decided that both she and it should be burnt. The nobles seeking to dissuade him, the king 'was content to spare the child's life, and yet to put it to a worse death'.

In the opening lines of Shakespeare's scene Leontes struggles with his weakness in bearing a manifest injury as he does. He can take no rest until he may mitigate his choler with a just revenge

---

entertained him with such familiar courtesy as Egistus perceived himself to be very well welcome, . . . [and] willing to show how unfeignedly she loved her husband by his friend's entertainment, used him likewise so familiarly that her countenance bewrayed how her mind was affected towards him, oftentimes coming herself into his bed chamber.

The second passage is at the exit of Hermione and Polixenes to the garden. Here Shakespeare's thoughts revert to Bellaria and Egistus, who when Pandosto was busy walked in the garden and 'in private and pleasant devices, would pass away the time to both their contents'. In this place he again recalls also Pandosto 'wishing his wife to welcome his old friend', and Bellaria 'willing to shew how unfeignedly she loved her husband by his friend's entertainment'; for as Hermione departs with Polixenes, Leontes with heavy sarcasm entreats her:

Hermione,
How thou lov'st us, show in our brother's welcome.   (173)

upon his wife, the harlot king being beyond his reach. Pandosto is a man of decisions not decision, and Shakespeare emphasizes this characteristic in Leontes by making him four times meditate, threaten or order burnings (ll. 8, 95, 113, 133)—thus sketching-in a melodramatic obsession which anticipates Paulina's later fanciful picture of Leontes as the stage tyrant (III, ii, 175), adumbrated here at l. 115. Greene's paradoxical way of expressing the king's change of mind about the child's fate (to spare its life, and yet put it to a worse death) probably gave Shakespeare the idea of Leontes' more obvious vacillation:

> better burn it now
> Than curse it then. But be it: let it live.
> It shall not neither. (155)

The image 'I am a feather for each wind that blows' (153) also may be said to derive from Greene. It seems that Shakespeare conceived a state of harmony between Pandosto's mind and the plight of his infant victim—in a boat without sail or rudder, 'left to the wind and wave as the destinies please to appoint' (p. 194). Perdita's lot is different—to be carried safely over the seas and left to the perils of a remote and desert place (173)—but in Leontes' state of mind in giving the order—'a feather for each wind'—it is Pandosto's command that is reflected.[1]

C

HERMIONE'S TRIAL (*W.T.* III, ii)

The court of judges is presided over by Leontes himself, who opens the proceedings, calls for the prisoner to be led in and the indictment to be read. Hermione replies, addressing herself first to the court at large (22), and then, turning to the tyrant and false accuser (31), speaks direct to him. At l. 37 ('For behold me, / A fellow of the royal bed . . .') she appears to be making her appeal general, but at l. 45 is confining it to the king's conscience. His interjected accusations and her replies keep the exchanges pretty

---

[1] We may recall that *Cymbeline* also gives evidence—at IV, iii, 46—of the impression Pandosto's boat made on Shakespeare's imagination.

personal for some time. Suddenly, at l. 114, however, Hermione
speaks out to the whole bench—

> Your honours all,
> I do refer me to the Oracle:
> Apollo be my judge!—

side-stepping its jurisdiction and appealing to a higher court.

Attention is concentrated on the innocent and patient queen
and, to a minor but sufficient extent, on her violent, vindictive
husband. Hermione has no witnesses (24), and there is no question of any witnesses for the prosecution. The shorthand of the
stage rules out that question, and also the question of a jury: it is
tacitly assumed that there are none, Leontes being a tyrant.

In *Pandosto* these questions are gone into pretty thoroughly at
the first trial, and it is because the queen can get no satisfaction
concerning them that she asks for the Oracle to be consulted. She
wished her false accusers to be heard in court, we are told, and the
judges supported her claim, adding that she ought to be tried by a
jury of her peers. Pandosto was outraged. Her accusers 'were of
such credit as their words were sufficient witness'. 'In this case he
might and would dispense with the law', and, if the court wished
for a jury, the jury would have to 'take his word for sufficient
evidence'. Bellaria therefore

> told the king if his fury might stand for a law that it were vain to
> have the jury yield their verdict, (pp. 194f.)

and asked that the verdict be left to the Oracle of Apollo.

Pandosto had called his wife 'for the more reproach into open
court' (cf. ll. 9, 41, 105). She, 'standing like a prisoner at the bar'
(cf. l. 40), and

> seeing that no less than death could pacify her husband's wrath,
> waxed bold and desired that she might have law and justice, for
> mercy she neither craved nor hoped for. (p. 194)

Shakespeare's imagination was plainly stimulated by details such
as these, which helped to define the attitudes of husband and wife
here, and, we should note, in II, i also. The effect of a stimulus is
unpredictable, however. It may set the imagination to work but
does not determine how it is to work. Thus when Bellaria asked
that the Oracle might be consulted it was 'fearing more perpetual
infamy than momentary death', and she fell down on her knees to

make the request. Shakespeare develops the queen's attitude to infamy and death, but as for the act of kneeling, he gives this to the cowed courtiers pleading for the baby's life at II, iii, 152, where as the unanimous expression of horror and revulsion it is impressive. Hermione remains standing throughout her trial, in keeping with her superior dignity and composure. In this case Bellaria's behaviour, if acting as a stimulus, operated in the contrary direction, just as Bellaria's tears in prison may have determined Shakespeare to make Hermione 'not prone to weeping'. The same is true of Bellaria's aggregation of negatives (fearing infamy more than death), which Shakespeare tends to express in more positive terms (standing for—or freeing—honour):

> For life, I prize it
> As I weigh grief (which I would spare): for honour
> 'Tis a derivative from me to mine,
> And only that I stand for.   (42)
> Tell me what blessings I have here alive,
> That I should fear to die? Therefore proceed.
> But yet hear this: mistake me not: no life,
> I prize it not a straw, but for mine honour,
> Which I would free: . . .   (107–11)

Gathering force and direction that last passage leads up to the well-known conclusion, which it is worth while to quote once more:

> if I shall be condemn'd
> Upon surmises, all proofs sleeping else
> But what your jealousies awake, I tell you
> 'Tis rigour and not law. Your honours all,
> I do refer me to the Oracle:
> Apollo be my judge!   (111–16)

These lines combine phrases spoken by Bellaria at both her trials. At the first she concludes a speech asserting that 'if she were condemned without any further proof it was rigour and not law'. At the second her speech ends with the words, 'and that this is true which I have here rehearsed I refer myself to the divine Oracle'.

There is also the immediate concurrence of one of Hermione's judges to be noted, and his call for the oracle:

> This your request
> Is altogether just: therefore bring forth,
> And in Apollo's name, his oracle. (116)

This may be said to conflate several similar details from the two trials in *Pandosto*. Bellaria's judges, as we have seen, support her appeal that her accusers should appear in court, saying that she 'spake reason'; and when the king refuses she asks that the Oracle be consulted. 'The request was so reasonable', we are told, 'that Pandosto could not for shame deny it' (p. 195). When at the second trial Bellaria refers herself to the oracle, she 'had no sooner said but the king commanded that one of his dukes should read the contents of the scroll'. Shakespeare deprives Leontes of the saving grace of immediate acquiescence, and instead makes this the opportunity for the law, through one of its representatives ('Your honours all'), to speak out for the first time and to assert its authority.

D

ROMANTIC LOVE (*W.T.* IV, iv)

J. H. P. Pafford (p. lxxix) remarks that 'There are few differences in the treatment between the play and its source which are more striking than the love-making of Dorastus and Fawnia and Florizel and Perdita'. Large differences are indeed to be expected, since Greene's narrative covers the earlier as well as the later stages of the affair, and since his habitual use of monologue lends itself to the display of self-searching and analysis on the threshold of love. Working in a single scene when the lovers have already reached an understanding Shakespeare can achieve a unity of effect and a lyrical coherence inconsistent with Greene's narrative scope and style. Further, Shakespeare can fill the stage and provide a setting of youth and song and dance, heightened in its effect by the contrasting presence of age, whereas in accordance with his method Greene deals rather in a succession of private meetings separated by long passages of solitary self-communing.

The strongest contrasts, however, are independent of form and style, and concern the nature of romantic love itself. In the play, as we have seen, young love manifests itself in mutual trust and

161

loyalty—expressions of individual integrity. Florizel is convinced that to keep faith with Perdita and retain her love is the one necessity of life to him; and behind this is his unswerving belief in his own rectitude and in his consequent right and power to set aside all conceivable obstacles to their union. Perdita gives him whole-hearted support; knowing herself to be chaste and true she credits her lover with the same qualities. Confident in himself, each is unselfish in his admiration for the other, and single-minded in his respect for the other's honour. Honour, for both, means dignity as a human being. The sentiment of honour is shown in Hermione to be bound up with the sense of rank, for ideally nobility of character and of rank go together. But for neither Florizel nor Perdita is rank a barrier. Perdita recognizes that the claims not of rank but of common humanity are paramount (445), but that has nothing to do with her readiness to marry Florizel. She is by birth a princess and by natural endowment worthy to be one. Aristocratically opposed to the marriage of a nobler scion to the baser stock, she is yet not conscious of insufficiency in herself on that score. We, the audience, know her to be a princess, though she and Florizel do not: symbolically she is dressed as a goddess, and he like a god come down to earth with amorous (but in his case honourable) intentions. Prince and shepherd-girl are not only equal but are seen to be equal.

In handling his material thus, Shakespeare is far more in sympathy with the young, more in tune with the customary postulates of romance than Greene is in *Pandosto*. In romance it is almost an axiom that lovers are right to follow their own hearts and to disregard the objections of parents—that is, when the parties are (though no doubt unknown to one another) of equal rank. So it is in *The Winter's Tale*: Shakespeare recognizes the strength and courage and nobility of young love in the pursuit of its end. But he recognizes also the danger it risks through its recklessness and impatience. So, in the idealizing mood of romance, he enlarges its scope by distilling from the rash and wilful obstructiveness of age its informing beneficent purpose—to prevent the young from coming to harm—and, identifying Camillo with wisdom and Leontes with benevolence born of repentance, he combines the dynamic capacity of youth with the guiding power of experience to their mutual benefit.

Like many another hero of romance, Dorastus is at first utterly opposed to love; but unlike other such heroes, he never really becomes an ardent convert. He is struck down by beauty's shaft, but it is 'an envenomed shaft' (p. 204). 'Beauty must be obeyed because it is beauty' (p. 205); but he obeys unwillingly and, though 'a slave to love', still struggles. He rejects at the outset his father's plan that he should marry the King of Denmark's daughter, regretfully and 'half angry with himself' (p. 203); and after he meets Fawnia he is constantly troubled because he knows that marriage with her will grieve his father. The fact is that he shares Egistus's scruples: the disparity in station is a derogation of his 'honour', that is, his sense of rank. He calls to mind that 'The gods above disdain not to love women beneath' (p. 206), and wonders at Fawnia's courtly behaviour; but this does not reconcile him to his infatuation. 'His honour wished him to cease from such folly, but love forced him to follow fancy. Yea, and in despite of honour, love won the conquest' (p. 210), and he eloped with the girl. In so doing, 'Dorastus little regarded either father, country, or kingdom in respect of his lady Fawnia' (p. 217). He has plenty of time for further oscillations of feeling, for Pandosto puts him in gaol while trying to seduce Fawnia. When she turned out to be a princess 'Dorastus was glad he should get such a wife', but in his last speech before that, while he is still in prison, we hear him complaining:

'Ah, unfortunate wretch! born to mishap, now thy folly hath his desert: art thou not worthy for thy base mind to have bad fortune? could the destinies favour thee, which hast forgot thine honour and dignities? will not the gods plague him in despite, that paineth his father with disobedience?' (p. 221)

The variety and inconsistency of motive which prompt Dorastus could have been used to betoken the tangled skein of human existence. But lacking the force of conviction in the writer they lose themselves in mere incoherence.

Dorastus is not alone in trying to suppress his 'affection' because of Fawnia's 'base estate'. Fawnia does it too (pp. 205f.). Rank is for her not an article of faith but a fact of existence:

Will eagles catch at flies? will cedars stoop to brambles, or mighty princes look at such homely trulls? No, no; think this: Dorastus' disdain is greater than thy desire: he is a prince respecting his honour, thou a beggar's brat forgetting thy calling.

But 'love is a lord who will command by power, and constrain by force', and she is unable to struggle against it.

Like Perdita Fawnia is clear sighted, alive to realities. She promises the prince that she can love him 'when Dorastus becomes a shepherd' (p. 209), but when he comes dressed as one (p. 211) she is quick to tell him that 'this attire hath not made Dorastus a shepherd, but to seem like a shepherd'. In what follows we can see, on the plane of bourgeois romance, materials on which Shakespeare set to work, with incomparably finer taste and delicacy of apprehension:

'If my desire were against law' [said Dorastus, concluding his reply], thou mightest justly deny me by reason; but I love thee, Fawnia, not to misuse thee as a concubine, but to use thee as my wife. I can promise no more, and mean to perform no less'.

Fawnia, hearing this solemn protestation of Dorastus, could no longer withstand the assault, but yielded up the fort in these friendly terms:

'Ah, Dorastus . . ., I yield, not overcome with prayers but with love, resting Dorastus' handmaid, ready to obey his will, if no prejudice at all to his honour, nor to my credit'.

Dorastus, hearing this friendly conclusion of Fawnia, embraced her in his arms, swearing that neither distance, time, nor adverse fortune, should diminish his affection; but that, in despite of the destinies, he would remain loyal unto death.

When Florizel says that sort of thing (cf. IV, iv, 35–46), we know he means it. But Dorastus cannot continue forthright for long. He will remain loyal to Fawnia unto death, but takes no risks in trying to keep her alive. Near the end he is set free at his father's request, is made much of, and put sitting in a chair of honour. There he is told that his father has also asked that Fawnia should be put to death. He is 'touched to the quick. . . . But neither could his sorrow nor his persuasions prevail', we read; and he remains seated, without further remonstrance, while Pandosto pronounces the death sentence, raging against Fawnia as a beggar presuming to match with a prince—'by thy alluring looks to enchant the son of a king to leave his own country to fulfil thy disordinate lusts' (p. 223).

Fawnia, in contrast, is altogether true to her word. When Pandosto offers himself to her as a more profitable lover than the mere knight Meleagrus—Dorastus's alias in his elopement—she replies by echoing the words of Dorastus's proposal of marriage: 'I am promised Meleagrus to love, and will perform no less'. With more truth to life than to pastoral convention, however, the shepherd girl's love is not without mercenary taint, for, having plighted her troth to Dorastus, she is anxious to escape with him to Italy,

> joyful, that, being a shepherd, fortune had favoured her so as to reward her with the love of a prince, hoping in time to be advanced from the daughter of a poor farmer to be the wife of a rich king. (p. 212)

Shakespeare is completely free from this bourgeois outlook. Florizel will buy no knick-knacks for his sweetheart, for she is not like the other girls at the sheep shearing:

> Old sir, I know
> She prizes not such trifles as these are:
> The gifts she looks from me are pack'd and lock'd
> Up in my heart, which I have given already,
> But not deliver'd. (IV, iv, 357)

E

CAMILLO, AUTOLYCUS AND THE CLOWN

Camillo plays a considerable part in giving unity and direction to the play. This is the result of his uniting in one man the functions of two characters in Greene—Franion, Pandosto's cup-bearer, and Capnio, Dorastus's servant. These are both old men, wise and loyal; and though they are of very different rank their functions are easy enough to combine, for the two appear in different parts of Greene's narrative. Franion accompanies Egistus in his escape from Pandosto at the start, and then is heard of no more. Capnio first comes to notice when Dorastus, preparing to elope with Fawnia to Italy, asks him to help. He,

> seeing no persuasions could prevail to divert [Dorastus] from his settled determination, gave his consent, and dealt so secretly in the cause that within short space he had gotten a ship ready for their passage. (p. 214)

Capnio has another function, that of delaying the discovery of Fawnia's parentage by kidnapping her presumed father, Porrus the old shepherd, and taking him with the young people to the court of Pandosto. There after many adventures the discovery is made; and all return to Egistus's country for the wedding.

Dramatic economy, dramatic emphasis on Leontes, and the restoration of Hermione all require that in the play the dénouement shall take place at Leontes' court. So Shakespeare uses Camillo to tighten the structure by bringing that about. Having persuaded the lovers to sail to Sicilia he goes to tell Polixenes where they have gone, so that Polixenes and he may follow. In this way the action will come full circle and the reconciliation will be complete, all the principal characters coming together in the last scene for the first time since their estrangement.

This variation of the plot unfits Camillo, however, for doing all the work of Greene's Capnio. Capnio meets the old shepherd making his way to the king and, scenting danger, he lures him to the prince's ship by pretending it is the king's, bundles him on board and himself makes one of the runaway party. These actions cannot be given to Camillo, for, whereas Capnio's motive is to prevent the king from learning of the elopement, Camillo is to put his own return to Sicilia on a legitimate footing by telling Polixenes of the lovers' flight and sailing after them in Polixenes' company.

Nevertheless Shakespeare sees that like Greene he must at this point prepare for the discovery of the girl's parentage and at the same time delay it. Hence he follows Greene in making the Old Shepherd resolve to show the king the proofs that she is not his daughter, and in getting him stopped and brought on board by a servant of the prince's. In a word, this appears to be the birthplace of Autolycus. Capnio's age and wisdom having been appropriated to Camillo, the quest for contrast suggests that Autolycus should, like his former master, be youthful; and the details of the kidnapping in *Pandosto* suggest that he should be a comic character.

Youthful, comic, a servant of Florizel's: Autolycus could well have been created as a court jester, a Touchstone flaunting his wit before a William and Audrey; and indeed the part does suggest such a phase in its imaginative development, and a reason for the invention of the Clown.[1] But neither Polixenes (to whose nominal

[1] Greene's old shepherd 'knew by his face' that Capnio 'was one of the

service Autolycus would presumably have been transferred) nor
Florizel, as the play stands, is given the mood or leisure to
encourage the courtly exercise of Autolycus's talents in that
quality. Besides, the stage representation of the court fool was
probably going out of fashion.[1] In any case, as the idea of the
sheep-shearing feast took shape, a more active range of versatility,
and indeed more rural propensities, must have suggested themselves as more befitting the context and equally appropriate to his
prime function, to kidnap the Old Shepherd. Some such considerations must explain the development of Autolycus (and his
formal detachment from Florizel's service); and to these should be
added the expectation that the part would be taken by a singer of
outstanding accomplishment, the excellence of whose performance is heralded by the servant who introduces the turns at the
sheep-shearing (IV, iv, 185–219).[2]

If the young Clown originated in the idea of a jester's foil,
Shakespeare must quickly have linked him in his mind with the
Old Shepherd, Autolycus's destined victim, who could perform
an aged variant of the same part. Hence as the Old Shepherd's
son the Clown joins his father in the first Bohemian scene, where
the infant Perdita is found. Providing comic dialogue and contrasting response he here takes the place of the wife Mopsa in
Greene. This device extends the contrast between youth and age,
and rids the plot of a character who cannot without pointless
complication be transported to Sicilia, where all characters except
the supernumeraries of IV, iv are to reassemble. After the entrance
of Autolycus, the Clown, meeting him, sets him off by contrast. This
varies the distribution of comic character and holds the rustics in

---

[1] The Prologue to *Henry VIII* (used for performances at Blackfriars) makes
a virtue of having amongst the *dramatis personae* 'no fellow / In a long motley
coat guarded with yellow'. There is a jester in *The Tempest*, of course, but the
unsubtle treatment of the part suggests that it is specifically a concession to
popular taste.

[2] It may have been conceived if not written to be acted by Robert Armin—
like the parts of Touchstone, probably, and Feste, and the Fool in *Lear*. But
Armin seems to have retired before *The Winter's Tale* was performed: Cloten,
if he took this part, was very likely his last role in a new play by Shakespeare.
(If the plan of *The Tempest* was sketched out before Armin left the company,
Caliban not Trinculo may have been intended for him.)

Court', and this suggestion Shakespeare delightfully develops in the concluding section of IV, iv, when Autolycus gets such fun out of playing the
courtier before the simple peasants.

even balance, for the father has perhaps the greater prominence, certainly the greater importance, in the sheep-shearing scene that follows. In the two remaining low-comedy scenes (IV, iv, 684ff.; V, ii, 124ff.) the Old Shepherd, the Clown and Autolycus all appear together. These are contrasting scenes, and together with IV, iii (where Autolycus so easily dupes the Clown) are diversified by the varying fortune, costume and bearing of the characters.

F

THE TRIUMPH OF TIME

Greene's secondary title is quite inapplicable to the story of Pandosto. His malady, 'the infectious sore' of jealousy, procured in the long run no triumph but only 'the death of his most loving and loyal wife and his own endless sorrow and misery'. Indeed we are told in the very first sentence of the romance that 'all other griefs are either to be appeased with sensible persuasions, to be cured with wholesome counsel, to be relieved in want, *or by tract of time to be worn out, jealousy only excepted*'.[1]

Pandosto's last act is to take his own life, 'calling to mind how first he betrayed his friend Egistus, how his jealousy was the cause of Bellaria's death, that contrary to the law of nature he had lusted after his own daughter'; but Greene by no means represents this as time's triumph over Pandosto. He never suggests that Bellaria's death is to be revenged upon her husband; in spite of Pandosto's hard and unnatural usage of his daughter, Fawnia is 'joyful that she had found such a father'; and his end is bewailed by 'his dear friend Egistus' as well as by the newly-married pair, by whom his body is 'sumptuously entombed'.

In what, then, does the triumph of time consist in *Pandosto*? According to its title, in the revelation of truth: 'although by the

---

[1] My italics. That jealousy cannot be cured by wholesome counsel Shakespeare agrees: it withstands even the advice of Camillo, later the 'medicine' of Florizel's house (IV, iv, 588) and hitherto the priest-like cleanser of Leontes' bosom:

> Good my lord, be cur'd
> Of this diseas'd opinion, and betimes,
> For 'tis most dangerous. (I, ii, 238)

But he rejects the idea that it cannot be worn out by tract of time.

means of sinister fortune Truth may be concealed, yet by Time, in spite of fortune, it is most manifestly revealed'. The text makes almost no mention of the operations of time, however, only of fortune; and it is hard to see much difference between the two in Greene's mind, nor is fortune consistently prone either to be sinister or to conceal.[1] Nevertheless the event referred to in the title as the triumph of time over fortune is the finding after many years of Fawnia, whom as she 'came by fortune' Pandosto had committed to 'the charge of fortune' (p. 193). The fact that her finding fulfils the oracle is, however, virtually lost to view, and with it much of the justification for the secondary title, since no directing hand is seen to be at work.

Greene's lapses are Shakespeare's opportunities. Adapting the plot of *Pandosto* in the light of its neglected secondary title he uses the triumph of time as a controlling and combining end, with the fulfilment of the oracle as its chief expression. He readily accepts as elements of his plot the death of the most loving and loyal wife and the endless sorrow and misery of the husband, but transforms them, subjecting both to the process of time. He sees that the 'endless sorrow and misery' which assail the hero after his wife's death must from the start include remorse for his crimes against her and his friend. In Greene it is years afterwards, at the end of the story, that a fit of remorse for those crimes drives Pandosto to suicide. This is when he has found his long-lost daughter, been reconciled with his boyhood friend, and witnessed the happy union in marriage of their children. For Shakespeare such a conclusion is unthinkable. He by no means understates the 'endless sorrow and misery'—cf.

> A thousand knees
> Ten thousand years together, naked, fasting,

[1] After Dorastus rejects his father's choice of wife for him—'half angry with himself that he could not yield to that passion whereto both reason and his father persuaded him' (p. 203)—we read:
> But see how fortune is plumed with time's feathers, and how she can minister strange causes to breed strange effects.

And we pass at once to his first meeting with Fawnia: 'It happened not long after this that . . . it fortuned that Dorastus . . . encountered . . . Fawnia'. Here time *co-operates* with fortune by speeding her flight, so that Dorastus, fated to yield to love, does so quickly. As he says to himself, 'Yield to fancy thou canst not by thy father's counsel, but in a frenzy thou art by just destinies' (p. 205).

> Upon a barren mountain, and still winter
> In storm perpetual—

but he conceives it as a source of spiritual purification and strength leading in the direction of not suicide but life.

As for the remaining motive for Pandosto's suicide, shame at having lusted after his own daughter, this lust was Greene's desperate contrivance for bringing Pandosto back sensationally and prominently into a plot-structure from which he had been long absent, and which was dangerously near to falling into two disconnected sections. Once he had performed the function of holding the plot together his sinful thoughts were turned to further account as a contributory cause of his getting rid of himself.

Pandosto is an unattractive character; after the start no attempt is made to engage our sympathy for him; and he has to be got rid of, for there is nothing left for him to do. Once he has lost his wife he has ceased to count. His daughter is found—by accident: Pandosto has nothing to do with it. This gives him a period of excitement and joy and a journey to Egistus's court for the wedding. But after that what purpose can he serve, except to give place as king to his son-in-law? This he promptly does by taking his own life.

So the logic of Shakespeare's treatment of the plot is clear. Leontes' saint-like sorrow can embrace no lustful thoughts. His looks of admiration are tokens of his continued appreciation of womanly beauty and virtue ('your fair princess—goddess') and of Perdita's strong resemblance to Hermione, whose perfection is at that point in the play a dominant theme. Leontes, unlike Pandosto, is to live on, and to have a dramatic purpose in living on. This purpose cannot be merely to be reunited with his daughter in fulfilment of the oracle, for, as the example of Greene's romance suggests, such a culmination could give a melodramatically effective close but not a dramatically satisfying reason for survival. The continued performance of 'endless' saint-like sorrow is, dramatically speaking, far from enough. It, like all things else, must be subject to time. As Leontes and his concerns are paramount in the play he must not be left lonely, with the young people departed overseas, and with nothing for him to look forward to but death. Hence considerations of structure no less than of theme demand the restoration of Hermione, symbol of his atonement, knitting up the great gap of time in their affections.

The Blackfriars theatre, and the question of genre

A

I

Referring to the last plays and the 'peculiar ethos which has gained for them the title of Romances', Peter Alexander wrote in a passage which has long been familiar:

> In this turn from tragedy to romance some see little more than a change in fashion to suit the taste of the Jacobean Court, more and more given over to sentiment and spectacle, and particularly delighting in the masque. This influence may have been reinforced by the tradition established at the Blackfriars by the Children of the Revels. Music naturally had an important place in the performances of singing boys, and the interior lighting might also encourage the introduction of scenic devices of a more elaborate kind.

But, he concluded,

> Shakespeare's Romances have been raised by the genius of their author far above any temporary conditions that may have suggested them, for they are clearly the expression of something he had very much at heart. . . .[1]

That was a very just statement of the case, and left the way open to further speculations in regard to 'temporary conditions'—while placing them in advance in due perspective—G. E. Bentley's well-known theory, for instance, concerning the influence of the Second Blackfriars theatre.

This theatre had had but a short history. In 1596 James Burbage bought part of the Blackfriars friary and immediately converted it into a theatre. Local residents objected to its intended

---

[1] Peter Alexander: *Shakespeare's Life and Art* (1939), pp. 200f.

use as a 'common playhouse', and in response to their petition the Privy Council prohibited it. Richard Burbage inherited the premises from his father and in 1600 leased them for twenty-one years to Henry Evans. He and his associates put in a children's company and ran the place as a private theatre. It was at first a success, but soon difficulties arose. Already in 1603–4, when business was interrupted by prolonged plague, Evans had inconclusive talk with Richard Burbage about cancelling the lease (Irwin Smith, p. 190). Thereafter the Children were repeatedly in trouble over the performance of politically objectionable plays, and after *Eastward Ho* (1605) they fell out of favour at Court, and for a time their theatre was closed. Eventually in March 1608, the nuisance continuing, the King ordered the dissolution of the Children of Blackfriars. Once more the theatre was closed. Evans surrendered the lease and in August the King's Men took legal possession. By then plague was prevalent, however, and there was little or no public acting in London before December 1609. It was in that month, therefore, in all probability, that Shakespeare's company started the practice of performing at Blackfriars in the winter season and returning to the Globe for the spring and summer months.

Bentley's theory was that the last plays were written expressly to promote the success of the Blackfriars enterprise, with a conscious eye on the audience and conventions of that theatre, and that this explains the novelty of tone and change of direction evident in those plays. He argued that the months from March to August 1608 were crucial: Shakespeare and his colleagues, expecting to open at Blackfriars in the autumn, must in those months have been busy laying plans. Shakespeare, he conjectured, undertook thenceforward to 'devote his attention to the Blackfriars and abandon the Globe' (p. 47).

That part of the theory has proved very difficult to accept. Throughout their first two seasons or so of acting at Blackfriars (which are all that here concern us) Shakespeare's company must to some extent have been feeling their way, and it would have been folly to neglect their large and highly successful established theatre, especially when in taking over a private playhouse for adult performances they were doing an unprecedented and risky thing. There is indeed no reason to believe that they did neglect the Globe. It was there that Simon Forman saw *The Winter's Tale*, and almost certainly *Cymbeline* also; and the presumption that these and the other 'last plays' were performed at Blackfriars rests on the hypothesis that from the start there was interchange of repertory between the two theatres.[1] *The Duchess of Malfi* was presented 'priuatly, at the Black-Friers; and publiquely at the Globe', and that, no doubt, was the usual pattern: dual-purpose plays (J. M. Nosworthy's term, p. xvi) are what we ought to think of.[2] Such evidence as there is suggests that in their early years at Blackfriars the King's Men put on new plays as they became available, at whichever theatre was in use at the time, and that special suitability to one theatre rather than the other was not a determining condition.[3]

[1] Believing that 'in the next few years after 1608' Blackfriars became the principal theatre of the company, Bentley cites in corroboration Edward Kirkham's statement of 1612 that the King's Men took at Blackfriars 'more in one winter . . . by a thousand pounds' than they used to take at the Globe. But Kirkham made that statement as plaintiff in an unsuccessful lawsuit: 'he magnified the profits as a means of magnifying his own losses' (Irwin Smith, p. 204). Certainly the Blackfriars superseded the Globe as the more important of the two theatres, but not at once.

[2] Perhaps better still, multi-purpose plays. For when they acquired the Blackfriars the King's Players were not confined in their performances to seasonal alternation between that theatre and the Globe. They had to be ready to adapt their presentation to conditions at the various palaces where Court performances were given, and to be prepared to deal with sometimes very different circumstances on tour—'within anie towne halls or Moute halls or other conveniente places within the liberties and freedome of anie Cittie vniversitie towne or Boroughe whatsoever' in the kingdom (King's Players' licence of 1603, *Malone Society Collections*, I, 264). As Dr. W. A. Armstrong says (*S.S.* 17, p. 204), the usages of the Elizabethan stage 'abound in variety and elasticity of method. . . . It is wise to think of such an age in terms of various traditions and syntheses rather than as settled systems of acting and stagecraft'.

[3] Professor Bentley included Beaumont and Fletcher, and also Jonson, in the enterprise, as enlisted in 1608 to write plays especially for the Blackfriars theatre. None of Beaumont and Fletcher's plays performed before the reopening of Blackfriars, and all of them for the next few years after that, belonged to the King's Players; and Jonson, whose allegiance had earlier been divided, gave almost all his subsequent plays to Shakespeare's company. It is by no means possible, however, to say that these were all written 'for the Blackfriars'. *The Faithful Shepherdess*, Fletcher's first play to be performed after the 'visitation' of 1608-9, was indeed given in a private theatre (Blackfriars or Whitefriars?), as is evident from the commendatory verses printed in the quarto of spring 1610 (Variorum III, 3, 11–13). But *Philaster* was most likely first played at the Globe (title-page of the 1620 quarto) in April-June

Professor Bentley did not consider *Pericles*, and this play has been seen as a stumbling block to his theory; but it may indeed rather support it. Registered for printing in May 1608, and performed at the Globe, it must have been completed some time before the disbanding of the Children of Blackfriars. Yet in coming 'To glad your ear, and please your eyes', its Chorus, Gower, may seem to announce a play suitable for performance at Black-friars—a dual-purpose play at a time when the King's Men had but a single theatre. The preparedness to displace Burbage's lessees which this may suggest would be in keeping with the course of his company's previous connexions with Blackfriars: Shakespeare and his fellows may have been watching the Children's difficulties with increasing interest, confident that under royal patronage and with a high reputation at Court they would themselves be far more acceptable now as neighbours to the gentry of Blackfriars than in 1596.

This is not of course to say that the prospective change of winter quarters *initiated* the new mood and range of thought and feeling evident in *Pericles* and its successors. These changes are to be seen as a natural development of preceding tendencies in Shakespeare's drama.[1] Nevertheless it is entirely possible that

[1] Cf. 'There is really no evidence on which to base a suggestion that he altered the natural process of his work to suit the new stage'. (Daniel Seltzer in *Later Shakespeare*, p. 164)

1610 (cf. Variorum, I, 117), and the first performance of *A King and No King*, 'allowed to be acted in 1611' (Variorum I, 245), may also, on the evidence of the quarto title page (1619), be assigned to the Globe. *The Maid's Tragedy*, on the other hand, was probably first performed at Blackfriars (title-page of 1619) in the autumn of 1611 (cf. Variorum I, 3).

Epicoene, Jonson's first new play given after the stoppage, was acted not at Blackfriars by the King's Men but at Whitefriars 'By the Children of her Maiesties Revells', between 4 January 1610 (when they were granted a patent to resume acting under that name) and the following 24 March. The play may well have been commissioned by them before they left Blackfriars two years before. *The Alchemist* was performed at Blackfriars, probably early in 1610, in which case it was likely bespoken by the King's Men during the closure of 1608–9. But there is nothing to show where *Catiline*, a King's Men's play of 1611, was first performed; and Jonson's next piece, *Bartholomew Fair* (1614), was acted by another company in an open playhouse. The only one of these plays more especially adapted to a gentlemanly audience is *Epicoene*, which was not written for Shakespeare's company. The rest, which were, are broadly similar in audience appeal to Jonson's earlier works, and, particularly, to *Sejanus* and *Volpone*, both performed at the Globe.

conditions at Blackfriars were congenial to their development. These conditions we may consider under three heads, audience, spectacle, music and dance and song.

II

1. *Audience*. Blackfriars was a fashionable neighbourhood, and the theatre drew a good part of its audience from the local residents. It was relatively small, with a capacity about a quarter of the Globe's, and as at other private theatres the charges were high. Each patron, therefore, both in his taste and his pocket, represented a larger and more influential fraction of the audience at the Blackfriars than at the Globe.

It is easy to go too far, however, in pointing a contrast between 'a sophisticated audience' at the one theatre and 'the groundlings' at the other. The Globe did not *depend* on the groundlings.[1] And though there was at Blackfriars 'an audience with some pretensions to cultivated sensibility' (Kermode, p. 152), there was a solid minority of others as well (W. A. Armstrong, *R.E.S.* X (1959), pp. 239, 240, 249).[2] These exerted a definite influence: private theatre audiences were by no means entirely dominated by sophisticated taste. *The Knight of the Burning Pestle* (played at Blackfriars by the Children in 1607) failed because 'the wide world . . . for want of judgement, or not understanding the privy marke of *Ironie* about it . . . utterly rejected it'; and the case of *The Faithful Shepherdess* is similar (see Beaumont's verses on the subject). Even amongst the 'sophisticated and courtly audience' at the Blackfriars there must have been various degrees of sophistication in dramatic taste; and the tastes of audiences at Court and at the Globe obviously overlapped at many points, as we can see from the plays selected for performance during the Court Revels.

[1] 'At the Globe, the playgoers in the yard are those of least importance. . . . Socially, financially, and numerically, they were outranked by the gallery patrons . . . who constituted more than two-thirds of the Globe's total audience' (Irwin Smith, p. 404; cf. J. C. Adams, *The Globe Playhouse* (1942) p. 88).

[2] Irwin Smith (p. 297) estimates that the top (sixpenny) gallery held about a quarter of the total capacity of the theatre—120 out of 516. Other estimates give a similar proportion.

Granting all this, we must none the less recognize the Black-friars audience, even in the early years of the King's Servants' occupancy, as socially and culturally more homogeneous than the winter audiences at the Globe had been. Relatively speaking it was small, compact and affluent and so the better able to call the tune, and this at a time of growing delight in the masque at Court.

2. *Spectacle*. The influence of the masque can of course have operated only very generally and indirectly, for it was a form of entertainment far transcending the resources of the playhouses in scale and grandeur. The masque stage, as devised by Inigo Jones, was something completely strange to the mere theatregoer, 'contrived out of Italianate devices—moveable settings, perspective scenes, complex machinery—and differing both in kind and degree from the sort of dramatic experience provided by even the most elaborate private playhouses'. 'The Nobilyty of the Invention', as Jonson put it, 'should be answerable to the dignity' of the noble masquers. It was a mode of celebration, not of drama: 'it is characteristic of the kind of action masques present that it can take place only in a world purged of drama, of conflict' (Stephen Orgel, pp. 3, 130, 17).

In large part, therefore, the Jacobean masque and the drama hardly touched. But in a more general way there was a good deal in the masque to interest the professional actors, some of whom had more practical experience of it in performance than many of their audience had. Music and dance are the constituents of masque, these and poetry; novelty and delighted surprise for the eye: the transformation scene, the revelation: the scene opening, the curtain dropping to reveal the perspective scene. Not much of this, on anything approaching the courtly scale, lay within the scope of the acting companies; but they had music and dance and good provision for pageantry when necessary;[1] and they were receptive to suggestion. In *The Masque of Queens* (1609) there is a long antimasque of fantastical witches; and this may have stimulated the revival (with added spectacle?) of *Macbeth* (1611), and possibly also the composition of *The Witch* before that. Whether they took part in that antimasque or not, the King's Men may have

---

[1] The most familiar instance is *Henry VIII*, 'a new play' performed on the day the Globe was burnt down, and 'set forth with many extraordinary circumstances of pomp and majesty', as Sir Henry Wotton related, and as the stage directions confirm.

supplied three of their number to dance as satyrs in *The Masque of Oberon* (1 January 1611), and if so Shakespeare turned their experience to advantage in *The Winter's Tale*. The influence was reciprocal. Devisers of Court entertainments, for their part, kept their eyes open in the theatre. In the statue scene Shakespeare gained an effect in dramatic terms comparable to that of a trans-formation scene in a masque, achieving the masque-inventor's object 'to merge spectator and actor in a single mimetic illusion' (Orgel, p. 188). Later the idea was adapted and elaborated, for purposes of novel spectacle and dance, in masques by both Campion and Beaumont.[1]

As for the representation of masques and masque-like episodes in new plays performed by the King's Servants in their early years at Blackfriars, this is rare except in Shakespeare. Irwin Smith (pp. 232f.) lists all their Blackfriars plays which contain shows of this kind. Of these only *The Maid's Tragedy* and possibly

---

[1] *The Lords' Masque* and *The Masque of the Inner Temple and Gray's Inn*, presented at Whitehall during the celebrations of the Princess Elizabeth's wedding, 14–21 February 1613. The double imitation gained point from the inclusion of *The Winter's Tale* among the plays performed at Whitehall before the marriage. It was of course already a well-known play.

In Campion's masque, two sets of four silver statues are 'transformed into women', providing partners for male masquers. In Beaumont's, an anti-masque of 'Statuas . . . attired in cases of gold and silver . . . as if they had been solid images of the metal', are given 'an artificial life' by Vulcan, and dance to music 'excellently expressing their natures, . . . very graceful, besides the novelty'. This is followed by a second and contrasting anti-masque of 'all the rural company / Which deck the May-games with their clownish sports', possibly suggested by the 'spirit of country jollity' in *W.T.* IV, iv. In this, 'the dancers, or rather actors, expressed every one their part so naturally and aptly' that the King called for it again; and those present, with others not so fortunate, had a further opportunity to see at least the same characters in action, no doubt soon after, for these reappear in *Two Noble Kinsmen* (III, v, 136ff.) to dance 'an excellent' morris 'rarely' before Theseus.

It may not be out of place to mention also the third of the masques in honour of the Princess Elizabeth's nuptials, Chapman's *Masque of the Middle Temple and Lincoln's Inn*. This takes for its theme Virginia, and for its anti-masque a company of baboons inhabiting 'a vast, wither'd and hollow tree'. (Two of these—'a He-Baboon, She-Baboon'—dance in Beaumont's second antimasque.) It is natural, though not necessary, to allow oneself to be reminded of *The Tempest*, and to think of 'the Baboonerie' as a proliferation of Calibans after the manner of the proliferation of statues in the companion masques.

Valentinian, besides *Cymbeline*, *The Tempest* and *Henry VIII*, belong to those years; and *The Winter's Tale* is a related case. Can all or most of the episodes in question be later interpolations? On balance, this is unlikely.[1] If they were later interpolations it would mean either that there was no great demand for such shows at Blackfriars at that time, or that the King's Men turned a comparatively deaf ear to it. But Irwin Smith calculates that 'in their eight years at Blackfriars, the Little Eyases staged thirteen masques or masquelike episodes in eleven plays', that is, 'in nearly half their plays' (p. 231); and it is reasonable to suppose that the King's Servants would seek to maintain this tradition. That being so, Shakespeare, in pursuance of that policy, was probably responsible for the masque-like episodes in his own plays. He showed no distaste at all for this kind of embellishment in his earlier work, when it suited the tone and tenor of the plot. As Smith observes, disguisings or masquerades relevant to the action occur in *Love's Labour's Lost*, *Romeo and Juliet* and *Much Ado*. We need therefore not be surprised to find shows of one kind or another in his last plays, plays in which visions and other miraculous appearances are in full accord with the mood. Satisfying the demands of his art he satisfies those of the audience as well.

3. *Music, dance and song.* The boys' troupes owed much of their reputation to the emphasis placed on music and song at the private theatres. This tradition was maintained at Blackfriars under the adult company, though music had been far less customary at the Globe. It is noteworthy that while 'the romances are, musically, the richest of Shakespeare's plays', the pre-Blackfriars *Pericles* and (as I shall argue) the transitionary *Cymbeline* are considerably less rich than *The Winter's Tale* IV, iii and iv and especially *The Tempest* where 'music is ... ubiquitous: ... and all characters are affected, even governed, by it' (J. M. Nosworthy, *S.S.* 11, pp. 64ff.). When he wrote these two plays he had obviously gained

---

[1] In the eight 'Beaumont and Fletcher' plays which Smith lists as containing such diversions only the two mentioned above are early; five probably fall in the 1620's. Similarly with the eight other non-Shakespearean plays performed at Blackfriars which possess features of this kind: none is dated earlier than 1615, and all but one belong to the 1620's or later. Irwin Smith reports that 'the incidence of masques in King's Men's plays increased markedly after the company occupied Blackfriars', but this tendency becomes clear only after the lapse of some years.

close practical familiarity with the musical resources of the Blackfriars theatre.[1]

Related to these is the increased use of dance. Because of their better provision of music, dancing was far commoner in the private than in the public theatres. Irwin Smith counts four dances in the thirty-three pre-Blackfriars plays of Shakespeare (p. 234). Four are called for in *The Winter's Tale* and *The Tempest* together. They arise naturally out of the spirit and circumstances of the scenes concerned and out of the musical terms in which those scenes are conceived.[2]

As a group the last plays have far more songs in them than any previous group of Shakespeare's plays. This may be broadly explained in terms of his own habits and predilections; for, since *As You Like It* and before it, he had shown a growing taste for song in comedy, and for some time it had been tragedy not comedy that he had mostly been writing. When a lighter vein returned it was natural for him to resume the use of song. Blackfriars stimulated the natural tendency.

'Mood music' had been common in Children's plays at Blackfriars. Its use was continued after the King's Servants reopened the theatre, and Shakespeare's last plays offer notable instances of this (Irwin Smith, p. 237). Conditions of performance at Blackfriars cannot have been solely responsible for that, however. If 'Solemne and strange Musicke' accompanies the apparitions in *Cymbeline* and *The Tempest* we must remember that the same mind that called for that combination had already presented Pericles as

[1] The probability is that *The Winter's Tale* was completed between 1 January 1611, when Jonson's *Masque of Oberon* was presented 'before the King' (*W.T.* IV, iv, 338), and 15 May, when Simon Forman saw the play at the Globe. It is likely to have been first performed at Blackfriars. *The Tempest*, performed at Court on the following 1 November, a few days before *The Winter's Tale*, was presumabaly a new play ready for the autumn season at Blackfriars.

If we suppose with A. M. Nagler (*Shakespeare's Stage* (1958), p. 102) that 'the King's Men simply moved their winter *mise en scène* to the Globe in summer' to perform a Blackfriars play there, we must include in the transfer the necessary singers and musicians, though presumably not also the customary opening concert peculiar to Blackfriars.

[2] 'Other dramatists for the King's Men', says Irwin Smith, 'were more zealous than Shakespeare in continuing the tradition of dances apart from masques'. But the non-Shakespearean plays he cites in evidence are almost all later than Shakespeare's, most of them much later.

hearing—in his mind's ear—'The music of the spheres! . . . Most heavenly music!' (*Per.* V, i, 228) just before the vision of Diana appears to him, and, inspired by Plutarch, had placed music of the hautboys under the stage—'Music i' the air.' 'Under the earth.'— in sign that 'the god Hercules, whom Antony loved, / Now leaves him. . . . 'Tis strange' (*A. & C.* IV, iii, 13).

III

It is evident, then, that while not abandoning the Globe Shake-speare did take account of the conventions and resources of Blackfriars, at least in the two latest of the 'last plays'.[1] Without the musical tradition of Blackfriars to draw on *The Tempest* and the long fourth act of *The Winter's Tale* could hardly have been written as they were written. The point is of obvious critical value, but particular rather than general. It does not account for the distinctive tone of the last plays. Nor does the taste for novelty which we may ascribe to Blackfriars audiences help very much: for though that taste might indeed occasion a change in a drama-tist's work it could hardly determine *this* change—a change, to the apparently old fashioned rather than the up to date, repeated in play after play. It seems rather as 'the expression of something he had very much at heart' that we must explain the 'peculiar ethos' which has gained for Shakespeare's last plays 'the title of Romances'. Before turning finally to the question of genre let us see whether there is anything further we can learn from the period of waiting before the King's Men started performing at Blackfriars.

B

I

Between July 1608 and December 1609 public acting stopped in London. But there was acting in the country, and there was acting at Court during the customary Christmas Revels. In the autumn

---

[1] For a valuable caveat against exaggerating Shakespeare's acquiescence in the supposed demands of the Blackfriars audience see Daniel Seltzer in *Later Shakespeare*, pp. 157 ff.

of 1608 the King's Servants were on tour. They were at Coventry on 29 October (Chambers, II, 214). Shortly after that they must have returned to London to start rehearsing. For during the Christmas holiday of 1608–9 they performed twelve plays at Court and received £40 extra payment 'for their private practise in the time of infeccon thereby they mighte be inhabled to perform their service'.

Next spring they were again on tour. The following Christmas, 1609–10, they performed fifteen plays at Court and received only £30 extra payment for six weeks of private practice, 'being restrained from Publique playing within the cyttie of London in the tyme of infection' (Cunningham, pp. xxxixf.). The difference between the two gratuities suggests strongly that the company had not been restrained from public playing equally long in the later months of the two years, and that their six weeks of private practice in the autumn of 1609 served the double purpose of preparing for performance at Court and for opening at Blackfriars at the earliest possible moment.

II

Now, on the title-page of the 1610 quarto of *Mucedorus* we are informed that that play, 'Amplified with new additions', was 'acted before the Kings Maiestie at White-hall on Shroue-sunday night. By his Highness Seruants vsually playing at the Globe'. In dating this event Chambers hesitated between Shrove Sunday 1610 (N.S.) and 1611 (1610 O.S.); but as it is certain that the King's Men were well established at Blackfriars by early 1611, that date must be ruled out for the Court performance of the revised *Mucedorus*. May we take it, then, that it was given on Shrove Sunday 1610, and that when the play was reprinted shortly afterwards Shakespeare's company was still 'usually playing' at the Globe?[1]

[1] On 30 April 1610 Lewis Frederick, Duke of Württemberg, saw *Othello* at the Globe, 'lieu ordinaire', we are told, 'ou l'on joue les Commedies' (W. B. Rye, *England as seen by foreigners in the days of Elizabeth and James the First* (1865), p. 61). But this statement of a stranger concerning the normal practice in the month of April throws no light on whether there had been a change of 'lieu ordinaire' of performance in the earlier months of the year.

We may not. The 1610 title-page of *Mucedorus* may very well be a parallel case to the title-page of the 1608 quarto of *King Lear*, which records that this play was performed 'before the Kings Maiestie at Whitehall vpon S. Stephens night in Christmas Hollidayes. By his Maiesties seruants playing vsually at the Gloabe on the Bancke-side'; and it is St. Stephen's night 1606 that is in question. It is very probable that the Court performance of *Mucedorus* was on Shrove Sunday 1609, the play having been in the repertory of the company's recent tour of the midlands.[1]

III

That Shakespeare was not idle while the theatres were closed may be taken for granted. Thomas Greene's finding unexpectedly in September 1609 that he 'might stay another yere at newe place' indicates, no doubt, that in his concern to see his company launched on its new project Shakespeare was prepared to change his plans, and to remain in London for a further period before going into at least semi-retirement in his home town. He is not recorded as an actor after 1603, and so is unlikely to have accompanied his fellows when they went on tour. The long delay in opening Blackfriars gave him the opportunity, therefore—this is at least a legitimate speculation—to plan several plays more or

[1] About the date of the Court performance there can really be no question. J. M. Nosworthy (p. xxv) gives it as 1607, but the alterations to the epilogue made for the occasion disprove this assumption. These refer to the cause of offence leading to the boys' suppression at Blackfriars (March 1608), and to their replacement (August 1608) by 'Men' of 'stay'd discretion' who 'eschew those vices' (ll. 46–58). Plainly the Children were still in disgrace at the time of the performance. They received a new licence to act in January 1610. Shrove Sunday 1609 is the only date which fits the facts.

Leo Kirschbaum (*The Modern Language Review*, L (1955), 1–5) is inclined to doubt the statement of the 1610 title-page that the Court performance of *Mucedorus* was given by the King's Men; but the alterations to the epilogue confirm it. Alluding obliquely to the 'gaules . . . So lately vented' at Blackfriars by the 'Boyes', the additional lines assure the King of the Men's intention to keep their hands clean in that respect.

The formula 'vsually playing at the Globe' presumably indicates that the 1610 title-page was drawn up before the reopening of the theatres, when the Globe was the only playhouse at which the King's Servants had publicly performed.

less together. That would explain the similarities and interrelationships of *Cymbeline*, *The Winter's Tale*, and *The Tempest* (noted *ante*, p. 4). It is entirely likely that one of them, *Cymbeline*, was finished in time to be rehearsed for performance at Blackfriars in December 1609 and perhaps at Court in the ensuing Christmas holiday. Amongst its sources J. M. Nosworthy (pp. xxiv ff.) has led us to number *The Rare Triumphs of Love and Fortune*; and so, in view of what has just been said of the revised *Mucedorus*, it may be conjectured that *Love and Fortune*, though probably not included in the company's touring repertories of autumn and spring 1608-9, was considered, or more probably, just suggested, for inclusion—thus stirring Shakespeare's memory while *Cymbeline* was in the making. This guess seems more probable than Mr Nosworthy's (p. xxv), from which, in part, it derives—

> that the demands of a sophisticated Jacobean audience, together, no doubt, with the prospect of acquiring a private theatre, made it expedient for the King's Players to contemplate the revival of some of the romantic comedies that had been popular ten or twenty years earlier,

among them *Mucedorus* and *Love and Fortune*. That theory incurs the fatal objection that once a romance goes down in the world there is no reinstating it. Rafe had played Mucedorus before the wardens of the grocers' company: the part, the play, were irrecoverably bourgeois, as bourgeois as Jeronimo, and could not be revived as polite entertainment on any level but burlesque.

The position towards which we seem to be led, then, is this. *Pericles* and *Cymbeline* may be regarded as a sophistication—in the sense that the literary ballad is a sophistication—not as revivals of the old-fashioned romantic play but as deliberate exercises in that mode, made from a more self-conscious artistic standpoint. *Cymbeline* may reflect in its tone something of the spirit of combined delight and mockery in which one must suppose *Mucedorus* to have been presented to James I (cf., in its very different order, Theseus's reception of *Pyramus and Thisbe*). The elements of travesty and burlesque that *Cymbeline* contains[1] find parallels in Antigonus's comic exit (though there the laughter is loving laughter), in the points of 'antiquated technique' in *The Winter's*

---

[1] Cf. Bernard Harris in *Later Shakespeare*, pp. 224f.

Tale noted by Bethell (pp. 47ff.), and in the deliberately make-believe quality that invests the conspiracy in *The Tempest*. Yet in each case the prevailing intention is clearly in accord with the high seriousness of the play's concluding scene.

C

I

Romance is an elastic term. It is useful, J. H. P. Pafford remarks (pp. xxxviii, l), to apply it to Shakespeare's last plays, 'if one is not too particular', for, in spite of their strong element of 'realism',

> they are romantic in true Elizabethan senses of the word, dealing with love in people of high estate, events controlled by supernatural agency and by chance, and heroic adventure in both courtly and arcadian settings.

This usage brings out their kinship with the earlier comedies, from which, however, they are distinguished by including sin and death, and by their emphasis on the surprising and sensational (cf. Pettet, pp. 175ff.). Again, in John Danby's treatment, a common element of Sidneian romance connects the last plays with *King Lear*; but in them, he claims, Shakespeare has got things finally clear and is no longer worried. 'The last plays are the fancies of Lear dreaming of Cordelia refound. They exist at a remove from reality. They give us a schema for life rather than the life itself' (pp. 106f.).[1] Lastly, F. R. Leavis has insisted that the romance element not only connects the last plays as a group but also—according to the degree of its success or failure in transmuting reality without falsifying human values—distinguishes them from

---

[1] 'The tone', as he says, 'is as important as the matter for a proper assessment of the last plays'. The question is how to weigh the literary intention, the dramatist's attitude to his work and to himself in the act of writing. His reply is not wholly satisfactory: 'I have myself no doubt that the last plays are less serious than those of the tragic period. *King Lear* is a religious statement. *The Tempest* is not'. There is a quality of lightness about the last plays, of artistic venturesomeness (which does *not* mean carelessness), but this must not blind us to the evident seriousness of moral purpose which informs them. Both elements are part of the literary intention, and jointly characterize a kind which is not strictly comparable with any other.

one another. *Cymbeline* differs greatly from *The Winter's Tale*. In *The Winter's Tale*

> What looked like romantic fairy-tale characteristics turn out to be the conditions of a profundity and generality of theme. . . . [But] there is no such organization in *Cymbeline*. The romantic theme remains merely romantic. Posthumus's jealousy . . . is real enough in its nastiness, but has no significance in relation to any radical theme, or total effect of the play.

With Leontes' jealousy it is quite different. It is a positive merit that

> In *The Winter's Tale* there is no psychological interest; we don't ask . . . What elements in Leontes' make-up, working in what way, explain this storm? The question is irrelevant to the mode of the play.

It is far from true that the play has *no* psychological interest; but the essential point has been made, that the 'thinness' of the characterization at this point in the play is not a defect, inseparable from the romantic element, but a calculated approach to abstraction comparable, one might say, to that used so triumphantly in the trial of affection in *King Lear*.

In *The Winter's Tale* there is, as Leavis says, 'nothing in the nature of a novel dramatically transcribed'. He finds *The Tempest* 'much closer [in its characterization] to the novelist's reality', and so 'a very different kind of thing' from *The Winter's Tale*. It lacks 'that depth and richness given, in *The Winter's Tale*, by the concrete presence of time in its rhythmic processes'. On the other hand, Dr. Leavis thinks, some readers may find 'difficulty in arriving at an unqualified acceptance of the statue business as part of a total unromantic response'. On this phrase we must pause. Surely the response intended is both unromantic and romantic at once: clear-sighted, prepared to face even facts that go beyond fact—the facts that romance is justified, that miracles do happen, that the humdrum is not the real world. There is no cynical comment here, no "Tis new to thee'. Leontes and Hermione possess their brave new world unchallenged. In the last plays, as John Danby says (p. 103),

> Shakespeare is responding richly—and with almost lyrical excitement—to the inward theme of the Romance. It is the inwardness

that is important: the externals alone would never explain either Shakespeare's excitement or the individuality of his accent.

If this seems at variance with Danby's 'unanxious' Shakespeare, who has got things 'clear . . ., almost cut and dried', then that Shakespeare must be set aside. For this is plainly the right one. Inwardness, engagement, individuality of statement are what count. As a descriptive term indicating mere externalities—types of plot, incident, setting—which might link these plays with *The Fair Maid of the West*, for example, the word romance is of no value, at all. Used, however, to imply the ideal of presenting reality 'with new intensity within the traditional romance framework' (J. M. Nosworthy's phrase, p. lxxx)[1] the term is well worth keeping as a label for Shakespeare's 'last plays'. This conception, which by omitting specific characteristics of comedy tacitly leaves the way open to deviation from that kind, gives scope for the qualities noted by Danby, and allows for the difference as well as the similarities between the Romances which Leavis so strongly brings to notice.

II

But romance pure and simple is hardly a recognized dramatic kind, whereas tragi-comedy is. In renaissance times, however, as since, this term could apply to plays of very different tone and character. There was the 'mungrell Tragy-comedie' of native tradition, unnaturally mating opposite breeds. There was the more respectable example of Plautus's *Amphitryon*, a comedy including gods amongst its characters, and so technically a mixture of kinds, a 'tragico-comoedia'. There was the modern Italian fashion of pastoral tragi-comedy, a middle mode, a compound not a mixture.

[1] Cf. M. M. Mahood (p. 150): 'Only the make-believe of Hermione, in playing at being a statue, and the make-believe of Perdita in playing the part of a shepherd's daughter, can restore Leontes to a sane discrimination between illusion and reality'. This statement does not record the true tone of the play. The extravagance of the happenings, their inconsequence and improbability, affect *our* reactions not those of the *dramatis personae*, tempering our engagement in the action with a mood of aloofness, not of critical objectivity but release from everyday factual compulsion. All is serious on the other side of the looking-glass: the looking-glass gives a special quality to our experience of what passes there.

And there was a varied assortment of dark comedy or comical satire or simply 'play' (cf. Allardyce Nicoll, p. 86)—of which only *The Malcontent* (at its registration) was actually called a tragi-comedy—all displaying a self-conscious if not always self-critical bent towards mingling the traditional kinds. Experiment of this sort was in the air. At the time of his own 'dark comedies' Shakespeare could contemplate with playful derision the ultimate fantasy of mixing the current 'big four' dramatic genres all in one (*Ham.* II, ii, 415), and yet within a few years was using something very like the 'tragical-comical-historical-pastoral' mode himself in *Cymbeline*, and (bating the history) in its two successors.

The pastoral tragi-comedy of Tasso and Guarini was court pastoral, and exerted little influence on English stage drama.[1] *The Faithful Shepherdess* is something of an exception and may indeed be said to 'prove the rule'. Like its prototypes, *Aminta* and *Il pastor fido*, this play is more poetical than dramatic. It failed in the theatre. Stung by its failure, Fletcher published it at once with a defence based on Guarini's *Compendio della poesia tragi-comica*, asserting that without critical interest and awareness 'this kinde of Poeme' could not be understood. Thus it came about that the Fletcherian tragi-comedy became critically self-conscious before it was presented in its typical form, and the potential taste for it which in the past decade had accepted Marston and Jonson and the problem plays of Shakespeare was given critical stimulus and fresh orientation. The new tragi-comedy, says Fletcher, following Guarini, is unlike the old, being

[1] *The Malcontent* shows that Marston had been reading *Il pastor fido*, but Marston is never typical. An anonymous translation was published in 1602, but interest in Guarini's play was academic or strictly courtly, not general. Thus it was performed in Latin at King's College, Cambridge, before 1605. In that year Daniel's *The Queen's Arcadia*, 'A pastorall Trage-Comedie', was 'presented to her Maiesty and her Ladies, by the Vniversity of Oxford in Christs Church'. Another pastoral tragi-comedy of his, *Hymen's Triumph*,

> Wherein no wild, no rude, no antique sport,
> But tender passions, motions soft, and graue,
> The still spectators must expect to haue,

formed part of a royal entertainment 'at the Queenes Court in the Strand' in 1614. *Il pastor fido* had

> so moderne, and facile a veine
> Fitting the time, and catching the court eare

that it appealed to the affected taste of the modish Lady Politic Would-be, not to the downright, masculine Volpone.

not so called in respect of mirth and killing, but in respect it wants deaths, which is inough to make it no tragedie, yet brings some neere it, which is inough to make it no comedie.

His shepherds, he explains, are shepherds of literary convention 'such, as all ancient Poets and moderne of understanding have receaved them'. When this play was performed, however, most of the audience evidently expected in a tragi-comedy laughter and killing, and in a pastoral recognizable country shepherds: missing 'whitsun ales, creame, wasiel & morris-dances', he says, they began to be angry.

Shakespeare had no such doctrinaire approach. What the audience missed in *The Faithful Shepherdess* he was shortly to give them in *The Winter's Tale*, yet without really compromising with expectations of 'mungrell Tragy-comedie'. Killing it has, but, more essentially, near-death. It has country laughter; but much more important is its emphasis on nature rather than artifice: it offers pastoral more 'Whitsun' than courtly in mood, and 'a Dance of twelve Satyres' that is mere 'homely foolery', performed by countrymen who, to look like satyrs, have 'made themselves all men of hair'. In so doing it probably pleased all sections of the playgoing public. Certainly at Court it was, as the records show, performed more often than any other of Shakespeare's plays.

III

It is customary to emphasize the experimental character of the last plays. J. C. Maxwell, for instance (pp. xxx, xxii), writes of *Cymbeline* as 'Shakespeare's first independent experiment in a new type of drama', a type 'that was entering upon a period of popularity'. To write thus may be to anticipate somewhat, for Fletcher had not yet issued his manifesto for tragi-comedy, nor had *Philaster* had a chance to achieve its resounding success. The success of *Pericles* can hardly be said in itself to have proclaimed the incipient popularity of a type. But it is experiment rather than type that Mr. Maxwell is concerned about: his final word on the play (p. xlii) is that 'there is something about it to which such general descriptions as "tragi-comedy", "melodrama" and "romance" do less than justice'. If that is so, can the question of genre matter greatly, since the play goes beyond it?

F. D. Hoeniger (pp. lxxiv f.), writing in somewhat the same sense, is more specific. He stresses the uniqueness of Shakespeare's Romances in the drama of their time:

> As tragi-comedies, they stand by themselves. None of Beaumont and Fletcher's plays . . . contains the most characteristic structural element of the Romances: the double plot involving parents and children. As the first of Shakespeare's Romances, then, *Pericles* represents a completely new experiment in drama on the Elizabethan stage.

In the specification we should surely include as a structural motif the importance Shakespeare attached to the final scenes of these plays. It is in the two scenes V, i, iii that the *raison d'être* of *Pericles* is revealed; and it is the quality of those scenes that is continued from one of the Romances into another, to be found in a concluding chorus of wonder that impossibilities have in spite of all vicissitudes proved possible and that what was severed has been knit up. J. M. Nosworthy must be right in his speculation (p. xxx) 'that the remarkable chain of dénouements which constitutes the final scene [of *Cymbeline*] was the goal that [Shakespeare] had before him at the outset'.[1]

What prompted Shakespeare to start this series of plays? On this question Mr. Hoeniger is helpful but not fully convincing (pp. lxxvf.):

> There was evidently something about the tale of Apollonius of Tyre that fascinated Shakespeare sufficiently to hazard writing a new kind of play. Working to a plot so very unlike those he had employed in either comedy or tragedy before, with few opportunities for dramatic complication or suspense, he seems to have decided to attempt something quite different. How can one otherwise explain the (for Shakespeare) unusual loyalty to the plot of his source . . .? If *Pericles* could not hold its audience by suspense, perhaps it could appeal to it by other devices.

These devices are the use of spectacle and music. 'The dramatist', he says, 'is deliberately aiming at an effect that is something else than dramatic'.

Spectacle and music, we recall, are indeed what Gower promises at the outset—

[1] It is not possible to agree, however, 'that he was content to tolerate crudities' (of his own devising, we must remember) 'for the sake of ultimate virtuosity'. These are part of the technically venturesome element which helps to lighten the effect of a serious play.

To glad your ear, and please your eyes;

but it is not these that make *Pericles* and its successors 'quite different'. The 'something about the tale' that fascinated Shakespeare was, it would seem, that like the story of King Lear it concerned family unity—suffering and loss in the family, the inseparably related fortunes of two generations—and that it brought the long-dissevered father and daughter together at the end in a scene of wonder. These are the leading features that recur in all four 'last plays'; the constant personal factors are the father and daughter, long separated in all but *The Tempest*.

Shakespeare appears to have treated the first two acts of *Pericles* as *given*—'good enough', as J. F. Danby puts it (p. 91), 'to stand as prologue to what he himself would add'. The plot offered a vehicle for the exploration of material which, he found, still excited him as a dramatist. The organic relation of parent and child had engaged his creative concern in tragedy. Here this theme was again, in a tragi-comic romance, side by side with a long-lost wife, returning as it were from the dead. But the rambling narrative form lacked inevitability of dramatic coherence. So, while the play proved a draw Shakespeare can hardly have felt satisfied with it; and he tried again, combining diverse materials, choosing a story out of Holinshed in which the king has two sons, and endowing him with the essential daughter (present in *The Rare Triumphs*) in the person of the wife taken from Boccaccio. These elements never really coalesced, however: Imogen never seems to belong with Cymbeline, nor is Cymbeline central in his own story. Lacking a permanent centre of interest the play sags: it has a splendid close, admirable parts, but the whole seems less than they. Wisely, therefore, Shakespeare turned next to a virtually ready-made plot in *Pandosto*—of which he had presumably been reminded by its reappearance in 1607 (though he used the earlier edition)—and tightened and sharpened it in *The Winter's Tale*. Then, having succeeded in the extensive treatment of the double plot, he set himself the further task of concision and, so to speak, simultaneity in its treatment. He devised his own plot, successfully this time, for *The Tempest*. In *Cymbeline* the king's wife plays the part of wicked stepmother, adding to the untidiness. Here there is no wife, good or bad: narrowing concision is the aim, narrowing and concentrating, fusing form and content, so that music and spectacle are truly structural as they could not be in *Pericles*.

Index

Adams, J. C., 175
Alexander, Peter, 171
Armin, Robert, 167
Armstrong, William A., 173, 175

Beaumont, Francis, 175
   The Knight of the Burning Pestle,
     175, 183
   The Masque of the Inner Temple
     and Gray's Inn, 177
Beaumont and Fletcher, 139, 141f.,
   173, 178
   A King and No King, 174
   The Maid's Tragedy, 174, 177
   Philaster, 139–42, 173f., 188
Bentley, E. C., 171–4
Bethell, S. L., 21, 73, 184
Blackfriars theatre, 171–83
Boccaccio, 4, 88
Brown, J. R., 16
Burbage, James, 171
Burbage, Richard, 172

Campion, Thomas
   The Lords' Masque, 177
Chambers, E. K., 66, 181
Chapman, George
   The Masque of the Middle
     Temple and Lincoln's Inn, 177
Children of Blackfriars, 171f.,
   174f., 178f., 182
Coghill, Nevill, ix, 11, 15–18, 122
Coleridge, S. T., 128
Cunningham, Peter, 181

Danby, J. F., ix, 184–6, 190
Daniel, Samuel
   Hymen's Triumph, 187
   The Queen's Arcadia, 187

Eastward Ho (Chapman, Jonson
   and Marston), 1, 172
Edwards, Philip, x
Evans, Henry, 172
Ewbank, Inga-Stina, 16, 30

Fletcher, John
   The Faithful Shepherdess, 142,
     173, 175, 187f.
   Valentinian, 178
   (with ?Shakespeare) *The Two*
     Noble Kinsmen, 177
   See also Beaumont and Fletcher
Florio, John, 83
Forman, Simon, 78, 172, 179
Frye, Northrop, 132
Furness, H. H., 113f.

Globe theatre, 172–6, 178–82
Goddard, H. G., 21
Greene, Robert
   Pandosto, x, 4–6, 10, 19, 21–5,
     29–31, 34–6, 38, 40, 44, 49–
     51, 53–6, 58–63, 65, 69, 72,
     75f., 78, 81f., 84, 87f., 90,
     92, 94, 99, 105, 108f., 113,
     116, 121, 145, 152, 155–70,
     190
Greene, Thomas, 182

JE

1 1 73